Our
Mother-Tempers

Pablo Picasso, *First Steps*. Oil on canvas, $51\frac{1}{4}'' \times 38\frac{1}{4}''$. Gift of Stephen Carleton Clark, B.A. 1903. © Yale University Art Gallery.

Marion J. Levy, Jr.

Our Mother–Tempers

University of California Press

Berkeley   Los Angeles   London

University of California Press
Berkeley and Los Angeles, California

University of California Press, Ltd.
London, England

© 1989 by
The Regents of the University of California

Library of Congress Cataloging-in-Publication Data

Levy, Marion J. (Marion Joseph), 1918–
    Our mother-tempers / Marion J. Levy, Jr.
        p. cm.
    Includes index.
    ISBN 0-520-06422-4 (alk. paper)
    1. Socialization.   2. Mother and child.   3. Sex role.
4. Family.   5. Social structure.   I. Title.
HQ783.L48   1989
306.8'743--dc19   88-36944
                                                                      CIP

Printed in the United States of America
1   2   3   4   5   6   7   8   9

For the Mothers of my life:
my Mother's Mother, my Father's Mother,
my own Mother, my Wife's Mother,
the Mother of our Children,
the Mothers of our Nephews
and the Mothers of our Grandchildren.

Oh, yes, and for all of us who have thought
our Fathers (or some other male) to be the
most important influence of our lives.

ON THE EDUCATION OF DAUGHTERS

The right education of this sex, *is of the utmost importance to human life. There is nothing that is more desirable for the common good of all the world.* For though women *do not carry on the* trade *and* business *of the world, yet as they are* mothers, *and* mistresses *of families, that have for some time the care of the education of their children of both sorts, they are entrusted with that which is of the greatest consequence to human life. For this reason,* good *or* bad *women are likely to do as much good or harm in the world, as* good *or* bad *men in the greatest business of life.*

For as the health *and* strength, *or* weakness *of our bodies, is very much owing to* their methods *of treating us when we were young; so the* soundness *or folly of our minds are not less owing to those first tempers and ways of thinking, which we eagerly received from the* love, tenderness, authority, *and constant* conversation *of our mothers.*

As we call our first language our mother-tongue, *so we may as justly call our first tempers our* mother-tempers; *and perhaps it may be found more easy to forget the* language, *than to part entirely with those* tempers *which we learnt in the* nursery.

The WORKS of the Reverend William Law, M.A.,
Sometime Fellow of Emmanuel
College, Cambridge;
In Nine Volumes;
Volume IV, *A Serious Call to a Devout and Holy Life,*
adapted to the State and Condition of all
Orders of Christians;
LONDON: Printed for J. Richardson, 1762;
Privately Reprinted for G. Moreton, Setley,
Brockenhurst, New Forest, Hampshire 1893, pp. 191–192.
Providentially brought to my attention by
Dr. Russell Neili, Department of Politics,
Princeton University

Contents

Preface

For all of my academic life I have believed three things about what we generally call *science*° to be most wondrous.[1] The first is the preoccupation with knowledge and truth as *ends*° in themselves. The second is the power, relative to the first, of highly generalized *theoretical systems*°. The third is the principle of *parsimony*°, which is as close as we humans can ever come to getting something for nothing. My interest in *social*° analysis has always been guided by these rather than by any empathy for my fellow human beings. I do not apologize for that; it is a fact.

The origin of this particular book is bizarre. In another connection I became involved in the question of whether legitimate *reduction*° of social phenomena to *puristically biological*° explanation is possible. On the one hand, most sociologists and anthropologists, joined by a rather surprising spate of biologists, maintain that such reduction is not, even in theory, a possibility. On the other hand, those who call themselves *sociobiologists*° seem to hold, in essence, that if explanations of social phenomena get very far as science, most of them will be puristically *biological*° explanations. Whether or not legitimate and elegant sci-

---

1. See chap. 1 for my distinction between the terms "believe" and "think," "speculate," or "doubt." Technical terms are italicized at first use and are keyed with the degree symbol. Definitions of these terms are to be found in the Glossary.

entific reductions can take place is a *metaquestion*°, as far as science is concerned, until and unless it is accomplished. We have in the history of science one elegant example: the reduction of chemistry to a special case of physics, of which the symbol par excellence is the Periodic Table of the Elements.

I have long believed that sociologists, anthropologists, and the like should keep an open mind about such matters and not deny, out of hand, the possibility of legitimate and elegant reductions of social phenomena to nonsocial explanations. Given the hopes or even the claims of sociobiologists, one is tempted to reply impatiently, "Put up or shut up! Do not continue to claim that you can do it! Do it! Discover and disclose an *elegant biological reduction*°, and we shall all have to take you seriously." It is not enough, however, to be feisty and quick. If one is to issue such a challenge to the sociobiologists, one might be expected also to give them something to chew on.

Given the general history of science, the most obvious candidates for legitimate reduction ought to be those behaviors characteristic of all *societies*° and hence, in some sense, of all social beings. And, so, for reasons other than those of general sociological theory, one's attention is turned to social *universals*°. These are not hard to come by if one thinks about the matter with some care, or rather if one thinks it is worth thinking about with some care. When one tries to generalize about human beings, most of what one has to say has to do in some way with *families*° and perhaps a bit with *governments*°. Within the realm of family structures, relations between *mothers*° (or *mother surrogates*°, who are overwhelmingly likely to be female) and *infants*° and *young children*° are a great deal easier to generalize about than others.[2] So this book was

2. In a sense, one can maintain that the family in general and the mother-infant (and young *child*°) relationships in particular constitute

conceived as a challenge both to the sociobiologists and
to those who feel that no legitimate sociobiology is possible.[3] After all, it does not seem farfetched to imagine the
possibility of a legitimate elegant biological reduction of
the fact that, so far, all human existence has in critical respects involved family experience, and all people in some
sense have been mother-reared.

---

what Merton might call the *Ur*°-Strategic Research Site (USRS) for
those interested in generalizations about any society or any *social action*° or perhaps even any *social system*°. Materials about families and
the mother-infant (and young child) relationships are, so correspondingly, what Merton might call the Ur-Strategic Research Materials
(USRM) (Merton 1987). See also below pp. 42–45.

3. This book is rather more respectful of the sociobiologists than of
many, if not most, social scientists. Nevertheless, it asserts again and
again that there are no examples for which sociobiologists have fur-
nished an elegant scientific reduction—i.e., a reduction like that performed by the Periodic Table of the Elements for chemistry and
physics—of any of the matters that are ordinarily considered explained
on a social basis. Some day they may be able to do that. Some day sociobiologists may develop an elegant explanation of why lions pride
and tigers do not and even of why human beings have families, but
they certainly haven't yet. There are some hypotheses about the
"asymmetrical investments of males and females in offspring." They
have some pretty good hypotheses about that, but so far no very good
reduction of any of the previously socially discovered or explained
phenomena. For example, there is an overwhelming preference in all
societies known so far, by females as well as by males, for male offspring. If one accepts the argument of the "selfish gene" in its purest
form as a *pathetic fallacy*° or as *teleology*°, one can mount a pretty good
argument as to why mothers would prefer to have male offspring.
Sons are much more likely to pass some of the mother's genes on to a
larger number of descendants than are daughters. One would have to
have a pretty sound explanation, however, of how mothers know
that, and how they knew it five thousand years ago, or what specific
biological mechanism determined that mothers would display emotional attachment for the offspring who spread their genes around the
more. How does the selfish gene accomplish that? One could go
through similar arguments about *fathers*°. It is also true that, economically, the investment of mothers in bearing children is much greater

Of course, books, like one's children, quickly come to have lives of their own. This book is no exception. What is said here of our mother-tempers stands or falls quite independent of any challenge to brash sociobiologists or conservative social scientists.

Although the pursuit of origins is always flawed by the fact that what we discover to be an origin must itself have origins, very general social analysis always leads us back in some sense to the family. All peoples have them, and, with very rare exceptions, all infants and young children are reared in a family context or in a simulated family context. *Eh bien*—where can one go from there?

Perhaps one of the oddest things about the bizarre patterns taken for granted by those who live in *relatively modernized°* contexts is what has happened to the place of the family in general *social structure°*. Before *modernization°* most people spent most of their time on this earth in some family context. That no longer holds, though even the most modern people generally spend more time in some family context than in any other. Indeed, what has happened has led many to think that it is simply a matter of time before human ingenuity invents various alternatives to what in the past we have thought of as families. Never mind whether that will happen or not. While the place of the family in general social structure is probably much more restricted and certainly wildly different from the place of the family in any *relatively nonmodernized soci-*

---

than that of fathers in siring children, which might raise some question as to why, if mothers really know about this, they ever have children at all, or why in addition to preferring male children they do not with overwhelming probability prefer those male offspring who are to become womanizers—cads, in the ordinary sense. Granted that sons are more likely to perpetuate a mother's genes (and a father's too) than daughters and that that has survival value for those genes, what is the "mechanism" that generalizes a *preference* for sons to mothers as well as fathers?

ety°, it remains the fundamental social structure for the initial formative years of the overwhelming majority, if not all, of the members of all societies.

I found none of the available material satisfying as general scientific analysis, not because the scholars who worked with such materials were inept or even limited but rather because our interests were almost completely divergent. Most of the work in this field has focused on quite understandable problems that "cried out" for "solutions." I was not intellectually interested in such "solutions." I was interested only in the question of what, if anything, one can say about any family system, any place, and at any time. I was confident that if one found any answers that were not true by definition, that is, that were not *tautological*°, the answers would have far-reaching implications for policy applications—applications that would be as available to the wicked as to the virtuous—whether one wanted them to be or not. I was also confident that such findings would have implications for further scientific reductions.

In this same spirit, I proposed the five axioms, and later a sixth, which are presented in chapter 2. I tried to see how far one could go with them in terms of the *structural requisites*° of any society and the aspects of any *relationship*°. I was literally exhilarated when I began to think about what, in a sense, all of us have always known throughout all time—that the initial socialization of offspring is lopsidedly asymmetrical on the basis of sex, that mothers are far more critical in these respects than anyone else.

After I had been working on this for a time, my attention was drawn to Nancy Chodorow's book (1978), which I discuss in more detail toward the end of chapter 3. In the first paragraph of her book, Chodorow states the essence of what I have formulated as Axiom V (p. 20), in addition to some of its implications, with a generality and simple diction I can only respect. I thought at first I had wasted my time. But it then became clear that Chodorow's and my preoccupations were two blades of a scissors. She tackled the problem of why women mother, a task I had put aside as too daunting. I am preoccupied, instead, with the asymmetrical maternal inculcation on all offspring of most of the *basic° structures°* of all societies. Her interests and mine differ in other respects: She is not as hipped on the general as I am; she is much more concerned with the implications, qualitatively and normatively, of her discoveries for women and hence for all people everywhere. I have learned much from following out her views, with some of which I agree and with some of which I do not.

I am more ashamed to admit that only much later did I read Dorothy Dinnerstein's book (1976). Dinnerstein does focus on some implications of what I have called Axiom V (p. 20), and she certainly comprehends and anticipates, at least tacitly, much of what I say here. She is more concerned, however, with the implications of mothering for human malaise and pursues these rather than generalizations that can be parsimoniously stated. Dinnerstein is certainly interested in—and interesting about—social analysis, but she is not interested in science. Much of her book hangs on fascinating assertions about the subjective states of individuals from earliest infancy. Often, though I think her correct, I can find no scientific basis for her assertions.

I owe the usual debts to the Princeton University environment that made it possible for me to write this book, as it has made it possible for me to write everything I have written for the past forty years. In this connection particularly, I owe a debt to Linda R. Oppenheim. She is officially the Woodrow Wilson School Librarian, but she is also the Saint of Bibliographical Assistance for all of us who need help.

Most of my colleagues have been too busy and too little interested in this sort of topic to give me detailed criticisms. Despite the protestations of my fellow sociologists, I find almost no one who is interested in what, if anything, can be said about *any* society. Jennifer Hochschild did give me examples of passages that were unclear to her in an early form of the manuscript, and I have tried to clarify those. F. W. Mote took time away from Sinology to give the kind of incisive criticism that is the jewel of most minds and a simple reflex of his. Marvin Bressler tried to save me from my stubborn, perverse malfeasance—for my refusal to speculate about "what it all means"—as he has for many years. Melvin Konner tried very hard to keep me from oversimplification and to make me aware of such empirically based qualifications as he knew from long study. Norman Ryder, a demographer's demographer who proves the relevance of demography for social analysis and vice versa, contributed the kind of criticism from which "you can run but you can't hide."

I owe special debts to Sylvan Tomkins. If he had had the time or inclination to coauthor this effort, it would not lack the psychological sophistication it so much needs. I have ever found the biologists of Princeton University willing to instruct the benighted. Among these willing teachers have been John T. Bonner, Robert M. May, James L. Gould, Henry S. Horn, William P. Jacobs, and John W. Terborgh. Special among them has been Daniel I. Rubenstein, a sociobiologist in the best sense. He knows what science is and what the social sciences are—and still keeps going. I have used him as a source on lions, tigers, horses, wolves, and also as a source of ideas about Homo sapiens.

Especially valuable to me was the willingness of Jerome Bruner to weigh in with his criticisms. Our association goes back to his days as a young assistant professor and mine as a young graduate student at Harvard. I sent the material to him fully aware that he would disagree with much, if not all, of it. But when was the last time anyone learned anything from anyone with whom one was in agreement? He has given me valuable, sincere, and carefully reasoned criticism to which I have tried to respond, briefly, in chapter 3. He probably will agree not at all with this, but I feel the work is much indebted to, even though not in agreement with, him.

I had the nerve to ask Robert K. Merton and Edward A. Shils to read a draft of this work and to give me their criticisms. Each of them took the time to do so. I think this book has profited from their suggestions, and I can only hope that their improvements of this work have in some degree balanced the distraction from their own. I similarly imposed on J. W. Goode, who responded helpfully and at length.

I owe a special debt to Marion Stanley Kelly, Jr., who in this, as in so many efforts over the past decades, has helped me in ways that defy identification; one could not have a more helpful colleague in another discipline. My association with Ansley J. Coale goes back more than forty years, beginning with his urging me to come to Princeton. He is still correcting my errors. He is above all the person who convinced me that demography was too important to be wasted on demographers. I also bow to Roger Michener, who is much learned at such a tender age. I owe a debt to Carilda Thomas, who strove valiantly to force clarity upon me and who brought special "up-to-date" insights to my attention. Finally, I owe a debt to all those strong-minded women in my life— especially my wife, Joy C. Levy, from whom I have learned so much—though they did not teach me why I have so seldom encountered any "weak-minded women," with so many of them reported to be about.

I owe another, very special, debt to the staff members of the Woodrow Wilson School, who helped me so much in the preparation of this manuscript. These have been, principally, the late Lynn Caruso, who did the bulk of manuscript preparation in its most inchoate stage; Lenore Denchak; Janice Finney, who helped so much, not in place of but in addition to her regular responsibilities; Sarah Jones; Rene Matyis; Joyce Mix; Sandy Paroly; Agnes Pearson; H. Schmitt; Nancy Thompson; and Penny Warfield. They have all showed great patience and forbearance.

Finally, I should like to express my appreciation of William J. McClung, who was prepared to accept the risk of publishing this book and who turned over the manuscript to two sterling editors, Marilyn Schwartz and Kristen Stoever. For them, editing this manuscript must have been like being forced to sit in a room with someone who continually scratched a blackboard with his fingernails. Never mind! They edited it with a spirit of professionalism and even a sense of humor that I can only admire. Whatever readability this book possesses is to be credited to them. I hope that will not be considered a spiteful remark. Their task wasn't easy.

I devoutly wish I could shift some of the responsibility for the shortcomings of this book onto the broad intellectual shoulders of those who have helped me so much. After all, they should have been able to overcome some of my stubbornness.

Marion J. Levy, Jr.
Woodrow Wilson School of Public
   and International Affairs
Princeton University
March 15, 1988

1

Introduction

ABOUT THE APPROACH

I try in this work to draw careful distinction between what I *believe* to be the case and what I *think, speculate,* or *doubt* to be the case. I refer to the former as *beliefs,* or *nonempirical assumptions,* or *metapropositions* as far as science is concerned. I refer to the latter as *propositions* or *hypotheses* or *theories.* Among the latter I include *hypotheses about the facts* as well as hypotheses as such. The object of this work is an essay in science. I do not believe that the phrase "social science" is an oxymoron—any more than are the phrases "physical science," "biological science," and "psychological science." All of the metapropositions on which science rests, as well as others specially indicated here, are placed in the category of beliefs. I do not argue them; I simply state them for what they are so that the reader may be aware of them. The empirical assumptions (axioms), hypotheses, or propositions in this work are all, at least in principle, subject to empirical verification or disproof, even though I present them as simple assertions. My beliefs are not a focus of interest here; the empirical assumptions, hypotheses, or propositions presented are.

The first of my beliefs about social science is that I regard human beings as a particular variety of animal. I do not believe the behavior of human beings to be separated in any *a priori* sense or by any nonreducible "emergent" or "immanent" property from that of other animal species. Not only do I not believe Homo sapiens to be separated from other animals by virtue of the possession of a "soul"; but I also do not believe that what we call "social" or "cultural" is in any *a priori* or empirical sense a permanently emergent property peculiar to human beings unless it is made so by definition. If it is made true by definition, I do not believe the resultant hypotheses to be useful for empirical, scientific purposes. It may be useful for the present, however, to take society or culture as *not* subject to valid or useful physical or biological or psychological reduction, *given our present state of knowledge*.

I also take as beliefs about social science the general metapropositions underlying any science: for example, the principle of parsimony (as opposed to the principle of *pleonasm°*), the possibility of confirmable observations and of generalized empirical propositions (hypotheses) containing variables arranged in sets with powerful deductive interdependencies among them, and so forth. In addition, I believe that no matter how convenient it may be at any given stage to take for granted that certain properties are not reducible to more general explanations, in sapient theory such reductions are always a possibility. Many elements in social analysis are not explicable on puristically biological or psychological bases, let alone on puristically physical ones, just as there are many elements in biology that are not presently explicable on puristically physical bases. I do not believe that such reductions, or comparable ones, are out of the question. I do not see in any such beliefs any commitment to any particular set of social evaluations. The possibility of scientifically legitimate reductions tells us nothing of the worth of anyone or anything—including that possibility itself.

However convenient it may be in the present state of our knowledge to distinguish among different sciences, I do not believe there are any permanently nonreducible differences between the so-called natural sciences on the one hand and the so-called social sciences on the other.

I believe that in science the number of constants and variables relevant to a field is not an inherent property of the subject as such but is, rather, a function of the state of development of the general system of theory whereby the subject is analyzed either explicitly or implicitly. In the simplest terms, I do not believe human phenomena are inherently more complicated than physical phenomena in general. Indeed, how could I? I believe human phenomena to be clearly and specifically a particular variant of physical phenomena in general and biological phenomena in particular.

I do not believe that the "natural sciences" can be differentiated from the "social (or, presumably, "unnatural") sciences" by virtue of the subjective involvement of the scientist with his or her materials. The idea that an observer's values and concepts influence what he or she observes and concludes is nothing but a special case of the general proposition that an empirical explanation exists for anything empirically observable. This is an underlying metaproposition of any scientific work. It is something we all believe, at least implicitly, if we practice science. It is, however, something we cannot prove scientifically. The idea that social scientists are especially afflicted by this metaproposition tells us that the person who so asserts knows little or nothing of the history of science. After all, it was not so long ago that the Inquisition felt exactly the same about the work of Galileo. Of course, he was forced to recant despite the fact that his theories were, for the time, both scientifically correct and fruitful. Similar reservations on different but nonetheless theological grounds were levied against no less a scientist than the great biologist Darwin himself.

There is yet another problem. The allegation that a certain social scientist says what he or she does because he is a male chauvinist pig or she a blind feminist partisan may well be correct. Such arguments may even explain why the individual reaches certain conclusions. The statement that what he or she says *cannot* be correct *because* he or she is a male chauvinist pig or a blind feminist partisan is an *argumentum ad hominem,* pure and simple. The explanation of why I say what I say tells one absolutely nothing of the scientific tenability or fruitfulness of what I have said. The argument that one cannot be scientific about human beings because one is involved with one's material is also simply an *ad hominem* argument. One of the metapropositions we do accept for science—that we do believe—is that *ad hominem* arguments are irrelevant. *Ad rem* arguments alone may be considered relevant for science.

The proposition (often asserted but never established) that human beings are inherently more complex than other parts of the physical universe, in addition to the *ad hominem* argument about our subjective involvements, are the two most often cited reasons for regarding the "natural" sciences as always a world apart from the "social" sciences. There is also a third reason—very popular these days. It takes the following vulgar form: "You are a man; you can *therefore* never understand what a woman thinks or what a woman does." Or, obversely, "You are a woman; you can *therefore* never understand what a man thinks or does." This is, of course, a special case of an *ad hominem* argument.

Such "reasoning" violates another of those metapropositions that one believes if one practices science. That metaproposition holds that "one need not be Caesar to understand Caesar." No scientist can prove this to be the case scientifically; he or she simply has to accept it implicitly or explicitly in order to do anything in the scientific realm. If in fact one must be Caesar to understand Caesar, it is quite impossible for any individual to understand anything outside himself or herself, and indeed she and he may not even be able to do that from one point in time to another.

There is even a built-in contradiction in this oft-asserted barrier to knowledge. If a man can never understand a woman because he has never been one and is not one, and if the reverse is true as well, how can anyone, man or woman, know that his or her opposite *cannot* understand him or her?[1] Furthermore, if this is held to be true, would it not follow equally that a person from the twentieth century could not possibly understand a person from the sixteenth century, that only Chinese could understand Chinese, that only blacks could understand blacks, that only Jews could understand Jews, that only Nazis could understand Nazis, that adults can never understand children unless they are currently childish or have perfect recall, which no one seems to have despite what we may be taught by psychoanalysts? All Marxist literature would be undone because how could one reared in terms of one class conceivably understand anyone from another, quite apart from the Marxist whim that class interests constitute an ever-germane independent variable? Clearly, neither Marx nor Lenin could understand anything about working people without this special assump-

---

1. This argument has an ancient lineage. Any Sinologist worthy of the title can tell you of Chuang-tzu's exchange with Hui Shih on the bridge over the Hao River:

"Chuang-tzu and Hui Shih were strolling on the bridge above the Hao River.
'Out swim the minnows, so free and easy,' said Chuang-tzu. 'That's how fish are happy.'
'You are not a fish. Whence do you know that the fish are happy?'
'You aren't me, whence do you know that I don't know the fish are happy?'
'We'll grant that not being you I don't know about you. You'll grant that you are not a fish, and that completes the case that you don't know the fish are happy.'
'Let's go back to where we started. When you said "*Whence* do you know that the fish are happy?" you asked me the question already knowing that I knew. I knew it from up above the Hao.'" (Chuang-tzu 1986, p. 123)

tion. The proposition that one must be Caesar to understand Caesar may be in some ontological sense correct, but it is a proposition one must abjure to practice anything outside introspection. *Science, by its very preoccupation with generalizations, is perhaps the least introspective of all the forms of knowledge so far distinguished.* [2]

I also believe that the heart of any scientific field is its general system of theory and the extent to which powerful deductive interdependencies have been established among the various elements in that system. Physics, I believe, is a much more highly developed scientific discipline than sociology, not because it is impossible to generalize about human beings while it is possible to do so about atoms or elementary particles but, rather, because the set of generalized propositions in physics that exist as falsifiable propositions and are not as yet disconfirmed is very much more highly developed than in the field of sociology. Above all that, the deductive interdependencies among those propositions are far more highly developed in physics than in any of the social sciences.

To be frank about my beliefs I should also state four others:

One, I believe (think?) most "social scientists" have little or no interest in "science" as I conceive it. Most have felt that "social science" cannot be scientific in that sense and should not be if it could be. Most have wanted to do "good" now or to understand "this" now and not bother with abstractions on very general levels. The very idea that one can analyze the behavior of humans in a scientific way is believed by some to be demeaning at best and

2. See also Merton (1972), wherein this question is discussed at some length, depth, and breadth—as we have all come to expect of him. Merton also ties the "Caesar gambit" through Max Weber to Georg Simmel. Without asking him once again to survey the "Shoulders of Giants," we may all wonder how much further back the gambit can be pushed.

downright wicked at worst. The lesson of the relevance of Newton's theoretical accomplishments has not been high on our list. When, for whatever reasons, such interests in scientific theory have developed, progress along such lines has appeared. This has been notably the case in economics and demography—both of which have gotten somewhere scientifically in the past few decades while "disciplines" like anthropology, sociology, and political science have grown more sophisticated only in their "methodologies," not in their analyses. Only in the social sciences is methodology a "field" rather than a "means."

Two, I believe (think?) that the "natural sciences" and mathematics have attracted and appealed to much higher levels of talent than have the "social sciences." This is happening for economics and demography, too. Perhaps it is necessary to get somewhere with theoretical systems before people have to have "Jacks or better" to cut a switch and enter a field. Perhaps a better class of talent is attracted to those fields that require "Jacks or better." I hope that belief does not rest too heavily on snobbery.

Three, there is a special premise on which this work is based that may very well be a fact of life rather than a belief. I do not believe (think?) it possible to discern the variances in social phenomena until and unless, implicitly or explicitly, one can delineate the common characteristics (universals) on which these variances constitute an overlay. If one cannot define or delineate the common characteristics of a set, how can one tell what subsets it contains? If one does not in some sense "know" the commonalities, how can one be sure one is in the presence of a variance?

Four, finally, I *believe* it is possible to generalize about social action or societies or social systems everywhere and at all times, and I *think* that the most general key to those generalities everywhere and at all times lies in the analysis of family structure.

ABOUT THE BOOK

The subject set upon here has to do with common sense. Everyone has known all along that for the first three, four, or five years of any person's existence, the mother is asymmetrically charged with his or her care and development. Where it is not actually the mother, it is a mother surrogate, who is overwhelmingly likely to be female as well.[3] Everyone "has always known this" to hold for all known societies: It is the common sense of all people, not just of social scientists, who sometimes ignore this. In exactly the same sense, all people have always known that when apples are released from a tree they fall, they do not ascend. This is true not only of apples but of most other things as well: Any individual holding a stone expects it to fall, not rise, when released.

What is equally a matter of common sense is to fail to reflect on the implications of this asymmetry of maternal care in everyone's earliest formative years. This book attempts to give some idea of the reach of the asymmetricality of maternal influence during this period of every individual's life, that is, some sense of the social structures so inculcated. Both the Reverend Law, whom I quote in the epigraph to this book, and Nancy Chodorow were well aware of this asymmetry. Indeed the Reverend Law pushed the fact much further than did Chodorow. Dinnerstein recognized the asymmetricality of maternal influence, too, and concentrated on what she saw as the most pressing implications of this asymmetry for women in our society—and, she felt, for most other societies, though she did not present her views on the latter.

3. Hereinafter, the term "mother or mother surrogate" (MOMS) will be used without the phrase "or mother surrogate" or the explanation that such surrogates are overwhelmingly likely to be females. The parenthetical phrase with its elaboration should, however, be taken for granted in practically every use of the term "mother." This is similarly the case for fathers or father surrogates (FOFS).

The implications of the commonsense recognition of this asymmetry of maternal care are overlooked in an ideology of relativity and "antiuniversals" posturing. The implications of this asymmetry have never been systematically studied for any and all societies. A colleague, Barbara Miller, in a review of the manuscript, observed that "the topic is important to a wide range of disciplines but has been quite completely and inexplicably ignored to date." This volume contradicts the commonsense neglect of the implications of this asymmetry. A hypothesis need not contradict common sense to be scientifically interesting. But any hypothesis that contradicts ongoing common sense, is not tautologically true, and is not trivially false will be scientifically interesting. Its refutation puts common sense on a firmer foundation; its verification overturns common sense. The ongoing common sense that this book seeks to overturn is the idea that what every mother has known and knows, every social scientist can take for granted and ignore.

This book, then, treads a knife-edge of common sense: It reasserts the commonsense awareness of the asymmetrical influence of mothers and other females (e.g., sisters) on infants and children. It attacks the commonsense failure to explore the relevance of that influence for the varied aspects of early *socialization°* or *education°*.

This study utilizes what is presently the most systematically worked out framework of analysis for a society and the most systematically worked out categories for relationship structures (see Levy 1952). It asks what some of the implications of this asymmetry are, insofar as one can maintain that they could hold for any and every society and could continue to hold for every society and every relationship until and unless human beings radically alter the manner in which infants and young children are socialized. It focuses especially on the initial inculcation of most of the *requisite patterns°* of any society or relationship.

Chapter 2 sets forth the five axioms on which this book rests, and it then adds a sixth. Seventeen hypotheses suggested by these axioms are also set forth—hypotheses that apply to all known societies, past and present. They may apply to the future as well; I think they will. Although the six axioms are presented as such, each is an empirical proposition subject to verification or disproof. As far as I know, none thus far stands disproved. The same may be held of the seventeen hypotheses. A great deal of work would be required to formalize these propositions, and that might require some additional axioms; for example, *learning*° does not vary at random to the amount of time and attention spent in interaction in general and in *teaching*° in particular. The rest of this work elaborates these hypotheses.

Chapter 3 fulfills one obligation of a scientist. It attempts to make clear at the outset the limitations of and objections to what is done in the work presented. It takes up some of the objections raised by those who have been truly collegial in criticizing various drafts of this work. I try in this chapter to state explicitly my position on these matters, even if it is a questionable one.

Chapter 4 states a set of generalizations about the place of family structures in the general structure of any society. The asymmetry of material attention and care is then followed through the general patterns of *role differentiation*° in chapter 5, of *solidarity*° in chapter 6, and of *economic allocation*° in chapter 7. In chapter 8 the patterns of this asymmetry are traced through *political allocation*°, and in chapter 9 through *integration*° and *expression*°. All of these patterns are present in any and all societies. Chapter 10 runs through the aspects of any relationship: the *cognitive aspects*°, the *membership-criteria aspects*°, the *substantive-definition aspects*°, the *affective aspects*°, the *goal-orientation aspects*°, and the *stratification aspects*°. In the course of this discussion, with regard to both societies and relationships in general, *patterns*° (structures) that are basic to all human beings are distinguished from those that are in some sense *specialized*°. No one has attempted this before. The attempt here may be tedious, and it certainly has not yet resulted in an elegant theory like Newton's, but it is a start: It is parsimonious, it is general, it is not tautologically true, and it is not trivially false.

Chapter 11 focuses directly on fathers. Briefly noted are not only the asymmetrical role of fathers but also the variability of paternal, as opposed to maternal, attention. Finally, I generalize that the major impact fathers universally have on infants and young children derives from the impact fathers have on the females who mother.

This book maintains, in addition, that although the learning during infancy and early childhood is not necessarily the most important, and is certainly not the only, learning one does (with the rare exception of learning like that of Mark Twain's cat; see p. 34), these patterns, inculcated on all offspring through all history by their mothers, constitute not only the overwhelming proportion of the original socialization of all human beings but also *that part on which all subsequent socialization is in some sense based.* All infants learn to walk, to talk, to eat, to sleep, to control bodily functions, and to interact with other human beings in a socially acceptable fashion overwhelmingly from their mothers, insofar as these patterns are socially taught at all. Moreover, insofar as being feminine or masculine is socially taught, such behavior too is initially taught by mothers, as is socially patterned thinking. If these patterns are not learned socially from mothers, little is left to explain their presence, save puristically biological factors.

Questions that are more properly addressed by people with relevant expertise are left open. Whether smiles are puristically biological or contain a social element is not explored. Stages of development—for example, whether offspring learn to use a language before they learn to use their emotions—are not discussed because expertise on these matters was not in hand. In the work available on such questions, however, the researchers seem not to have explored the relevance of their findings to any and all infants. Rather, they seem content to generalize from (or about) the subjects at their disposal. In many of these cases, the differences that would be made are not necessarily great, but where is there a systematic attempt to explore such questions for any society? They should be explored if one values science in these fields. Others with the relevant expertise may be moved to ask, more generally and with more power than hitherto, which of these developing behaviors can at the present stage of knowledge be explained as puristically biological and which ones still can be explained only by maternally inculcated socialization. One also hopes that someone will go much further and much more scientifically into Chodorow's question about why mothers mother.

This book maintains that mothers inculcate things on which all subsequent learning is based and that little, if any, subsequent learning varies at random to that inculcation. These views are quite at variance with views that maternal influence during infancy and early childhood is the independent, necessary, and sufficient condition for explaining everything individuals do subsequently. That is nonsense, of course. It is not nonsense to think that, insofar as the basis for human behavior is socially learned, it is initially learned in family contexts from mothers.

Prior to the modernization that began in the nineteenth century in a restricted number of societies (N.B.: not in the West generally!), the overwhelming majority of all human beings operated in some family context the overwhelming majority of their time. If one asked them about things from their point of view, they might well have said any substantial amount of time spent outside that context was "disproportionate." Even in our most modern societies, most human beings spend more time in some sort of family context than in any other single social context. Social scientists today do not generally attribute nearly as much relevance to initial socialization and the form it takes as this book does. Initial socialization with regard to various sex-role stereotypes is in many circles today overwhelmingly thought to be a function of male inculcation of patterns. Perhaps many would like to have it that way, but that is almost certainly not the way things are or ever have been for Homo sapiens or perhaps for other primates either. Professor Hrdy (1981, p. 201) refers to Jane Lancaster's (1973) emphasis "that female matrilines formed the core of many primate troops and that it was primarily females who transmitted knowledge between generations."

Some hold fathers to be important for the socialization of their children, especially their male children, out of all proportion to the time spent with them. Whatever is the evidence for such a generalization? It is a special form of the "quality time" argument: "Fathers may not be there much, but when they are, they really count!" Given the importance of close attention and constant reiteration for human infants, one may well be skeptical. One might wonder more particularly, when they are presumed to be important for sexual differentiation and the like, that male "quality time" is regarded as especially important for what males learn as opposed to what females learn. What built-in mechanism would lead infant males to realize that what their fathers or other males do is more significant to them than it is to females, or that it is more significant than what females do with (to) them? And why on earth would female infants not recognize it as similarly important? By what mechanism or criterion would male infants recognize paternal deeds as "disproportionately" relevant? If the time spent during these formative years is as asymmetrical as I suggest, then such "special" male influence must be a function of what mothers attribute to fathers while teaching and handling infants and children. Alternative explanations can be only puristically biological interpretations, or a sort of "deep calling to deep" mysticism.

A brilliant student at the Woodrow Wilson School who has himself tried carefully to follow a path of equal "parenting" (no one rears children anymore!) attacked the idea that young boys learn to be masculine, insofar as they learn it, initially from their mothers. He wanted to know whether, if one parent knew a lot about mechanics and the other knew nothing, one could say that the mechanical parent was overwhelmingly important in the child's learning about mechanics, even if that parent spent relatively little time with the child. As stated, indeed one could. But sexual stereotypes and the like are not matters about which one parent knows something and the other nothing. Mothers know a great deal about sex roles of both types, and inculcate them on children. Certainly by the time they reach the age of three, four, or five, children distinguish themselves as boys or girls. Even casual observers can distinguish their sex by their behavior, appearance, and so forth.

Furthermore, the mothers toilet train the infants, and that process is different for boys than for girls. Mothers also teach infants language, and no language is devoid of sexual distinctions or references. Those who are interested in them sometimes can find them in curious places, such as the distinction between "history" and "herstory." This must have started as a joke but has become a ritualized observance about implicit bigotry, although the linguistic origin of the term "history" would seem to have little to do with the possessive masculine pronoun in English, however effective a pun it makes.

That others also inculcate much on individuals is hardly open to doubt and certainly not contradicted here. Those who taught John Von Neumann physics and math were almost certainly more important in explaining his substantive knowledge of these disciplines than was his mother. The question remains, however: Were they as "relevant" to Von Neumann, the physicist and mathematician (apart from the substantive input of those fields), as his mother and himself? To what extent, where literacy is stressed, are "reading readiness" and "reading pleasure" functions of *mother-time°* by contrast with *father-time°*? If one shows that Von Neumann's mother was relatively unimportant in this, one is likely to be driven back on more purely genetic explanations for his genius. Oskar Morgenstern maintained that some serious and able biologists seriously speculated that Von Neumann's genius constituted a special mutation.

If the initial inculcation of all patterns dealing with the general structural aspects of any society or relationship— if the original learned forms or those on which all subsequent learning is somehow based—vary at random to the mother's initial asymmetrical attention to offspring, what can one say? One need not claim that the relative importance of families and things associated with families derives from the mother's overwhelming influence in initial socialization of all infants and young children. It may, but that claim smacks of teleology.

Two of the several axioms on which this book rests are that (1) there are no societies that do not have families as subsystems and (2) there are no societies whose infants and young children are not overwhelmingly reared in some family context. These statements may be truisms— they should, in fact, be truisms—but one could never in-

fer this from the way most social analysis is written. Indeed, the further implications of Freud's great contribution (however much one may argue the details) that
erotic life predates puberty is more or less ignored in
other contexts. The inculcation of economic and political
roles does not wait in the wings until early childhood has
passed. It clearly begins in infancy and *early childhood*° and
is overwhelmingly conveyed by mothers.

The mountain of new material about women and men
raises a serious question of how much current or future
developments are likely to invalidate the hypotheses presented in this book. Will a radical *change*° in child-rearing
patterns make a difference? Certainly it may, depending
on which patterns change. Conversely, if one asks
whether those changes are likely, that is quite another
question. Patterns of equal parenting are not nearly universal and do not promise to become so. Where they are
most ardently attempted, they frequently fall far short of
the mark. In most quarters they are not even ardently attempted, though in some they are ardently lip-serviced.
Often, the new patterns of parenting result in increased
use of mother surrogates who are, of course, usually female. If children were not breast-fed, however, and all
were tended equally by males and females, not by some
other female when both parents were away or busy, then
one would certainly expect one of two results: (1) a new
breed of humans, as when Theodore Schneirla discovered
how to rear kittens without the presence of any other cat,
perhaps viable, perhaps not; or (2) few or no differences,
probably meaning (a) that a larger number of things are
determined in the narrow, biologistic sense than most social scientists are presently prepared to grant, or (b) that
the male/female distinction, which is so important a predictor of so many things, has few if any implications for
the initial socialization of offspring. If that last hypothesis could be demonstrated, it would constitute a major

breakthrough in the social sciences. Simple assertion is not persuasive in any of these cases.

In every other mammalian species, the female of the species is in some sense asymmetrically attentive in the rearing (not to say socialization) of the young of both sexes. Would it not be fascinating if future humans put an end to the predominance of maternal attentiveness in their own species and survived?

2

The Seed

Male dominance has been both an *ideal*° pattern and an *actual*° pattern for the overwhelming majority of the members of all known societies, including so-called modern societies. Whether such patterns are "necessary," let alone "proper," "healthy," or "good," is outside the bounds of this study. Also beside the point for the moment is any discussion of how closely the actual patterns of a society approach the ideal patterns. Instead, here are some axioms and hypotheses about all societies regarding the actual role of women in shaping and perpetuating both the ideal and actual patterns of the society. First, the axioms:

    I. All human societies are characterized by the existence of family systems, and ideally and actually all the members of any society are members of some family system(s) (or some simulated family system[s]).

    II. From birth until the age of at least three, four, or five,[1] all infants and young children of all societies are reared in a family (or simulated family) context.

---

1. The question may well be raised as to why I stress the period between birth and the age of three, four, or five. It is, of course, trivial to point out that the period from birth to any future age is in some sense the initial part of any experience other than that *in utero,* but why pick, say, three, four, or five as the upper limit of attention here? If pushed on the matter, I would be prepared to settle for three, without its having much effect, I think, on the hypotheses presented here. The

III. The initial part of the learning[2] curve for humans, the part that forms the basis for all later learning, occurs between birth and the age of three, four, or five.

IV. All infants are and have been treated differently from birth onward according to their *sex*.°[3] By the age of

---

upper limit of five has been chosen for quite another reason. The analysis and set of hypotheses presented here are focused on what can be alleged to hold for *any* society, past and present at least, and perhaps, but by no means as certainly, for the future. Even for the past and present, however, what happens in family contexts to children from age five on varies much more widely than what happens before. That is certainly true for the matters discussed in this book. Especially with regard to sons, fathers in the past took a far more active caring and supervisory role from the age of five on. Even so, fathers vary much more than mothers with regard to how much they are in the presence of children and in what and how much they do for them when they are present. In modern societies, matters vary from the past in wildly different respects. Beyond some early-childhood age, certainly beyond the age of five, analysis across the board is much more difficult at the present state of our knowledge, and one is forced to lower levels of generality.

The period following infancy up through the age of three, four, or five years will be called early childhood here. Children of these ages will be called young children.

2. The concept of learning is defined here as any increase in storage in the memory of an individual, combined with the ability to recall that which is stored. This work is mostly concerned with social learning, that is, any learning not adequately explicable at the present stage of our knowledge in terms of the species' (in this case, human) heredity and the nonspecies' (in this case, nonhuman) environment. Puristically biological learning would, for these purposes, be adequately explicable in terms of human heredity and the nonhuman environment. *Social learning*° at some remove or other always involves interaction with another representative of the species, in this case at least one other human being. Puristically biological learning need not.

3. Throughout this work the term "sex" is used for what is elsewhere now fashionably termed "gender." I find the newer usage supported by nothing save an easily understandable strain toward euphemism in sensitive contexts.

three, four, or five, socially expected male or female behavior can be clearly distinguished by the child in him or
herself and by those with whom the child comes into
contact.

V. From birth until the age of three, four, or five, an
infant or young child spends most of his or her time under the direct care and supervision of an older female,
who is generally the mother but may be a mother surrogate. In fact, the ratio of female supervision, direct handling, control, and care of the infant to male supervision,
and so forth, is highly asymmetrical. The ratio is probably at least 19 to 1, or in percentage terms 95 percent to 5
percent.[4]

These five statements are presented as axioms because
they cannot be proved, but they could conceivably be
disproved by counter-example. There are presently no
accepted data on any society that contradict these axioms
as stated. From these five axioms, one can infer the following:

The overwhelming proportion of all infants initially
learn from their mothers the socially acceptable behaviors
and patterns for the following:

1. Walking

2. Talking, using a language. (When males and females
have different forms of speech, the individual initially

4. The ratio of 19 to 1 (or 95 percent to 5 percent) is chosen arbitrarily as a convenient metaphor. It could equally reasonably have
been given as 20 to 1 or 15 to 1. The important hypothesis is that the
ratio is wildly asymmetrical—not just a little bit. It has never ap-
proached 1 to 1 for the members of any society as a whole, nor has the
direction of the asymmetry ever been reversed. Any close approach to
equality or any reversal of this ratio for any peoples as a whole would
call into question or invalidate the central thesis of this study.

learns the patterns deemed socially appropriate to his or her sex from his or her mother.)

3. Eating

4. Sleeping

5. Controlling bodily functions

6. Interacting with other human beings

7. Thinking

8. Displaying (or refraining from displaying) *emotions*° and reacting to emotions

9. Patterns of role differentiation

10. Patterns of solidarity

11. Patterns of economic allocation

12. Patterns of political allocation, including some that do not involve their mothers

13. Patterns of integration and expression

Finally, two universal conclusions of special note:

14. To the extent that "being feminine" is socially learned, female infants initially learn to "behave like females" from their mothers.

15. To the extent that "being masculine" is socially learned, male infants initially learn to "behave like males" from their mothers.

Two hypotheses about the role of fathers in any society may be added with the inclusion of a final axiom. The axiom is as follows:

VI. Regardless of the role of fathers in infant and childhood learning, a father is likely to be present in a family context a substantial part of most days—even in the most modernized of contexts (see pp. 44–45).

The two hypotheses are:

16. Infants initially learn about males in general and fathers in particular via their mothers' subjective view of what fathers are like.

17. Because a father is likely to be present and observed in a family context a good part of many days, an infant's subjective view of a father is likely to be an amalgam of a mother's subjective view and that infant's observation of and interaction with a father.

The remainder of this book pursues these six axioms and explores their relevance to everyone's initial learning about the structures of societies and of relationships generally.

The salient point here is the asymmetric significance of females during an infant's earliest, most formative period. This is true not only for the overwhelming proportion of all who have ever lived but also for the overwhelming proportion of those living today. The asymmetric significance of females presumably would not apply to those factors in human development that (1) can be shown to be unaffected by learning that takes place in the first few years, (2) vary at random to patterns of initial socialization, or (3) vary at random to the amount of time or attention devoted to infants and young children—if indeed such patterns exist.

For all other factors, the introduction to, and initial socialization (or *culturalization*°) in, the ideal and actual patterns is carried out overwhelmingly by females rather than males. Freud seems to maintain that the superego figure is male. If this is true, it is because mothers have inculcated this on infants and young children. To put the matter informally, it is mothers who have said to infants, "Don't go out of the cave. The saber-toothed tiger will get you!" "You can't talk that way to him. He's your father!" "Come home with your shield or on it!" Only mothers bear children. We may also observe with virtually equal certainty that mothers form them as human beings. This, of course, as Thorstein Veblen would say, tells us nothing of whether human beings are formed well, badly, or indifferently. There exists so far no sound scientific explanation for why mothers behave so.

3

Peccator Forte

The physicist Richard P. Feynman has written a very funny book (1985), which manages to discuss quite serious topics with an unfaltering sense of humor. In the chapter entitled "Cargo-Cult Science" (pp. 338–46), Feynman discusses one of the fundamental responsibilities of an ordinary, as distinguished from a cargo-cult, scientist. The ordinary scientist, he says, is obligated to raise any questions that might throw doubt on his or her ideas. I intend to raise such questions in this chapter, though I may not live up to Feynman's ideal that one must "try to give *all* of the information to help others to judge the value of your contribution; not just the information that leads to judgment in one particular direction or another" (p. 341).

This book attempts to derive far-reaching implications from a small number of *empirical°* allegations. Abstraction is at the highest (i.e., the most general) level vis-à-vis the concept of societies. In science, abstraction is not some sort of evil with which one wrestles, Jacob-like. It is now fashionable for some avant-garde practitioners (Alexander 1982, p. 3) of sociology to regard "abstraction" as, in some sense, a term that stands in polar opposition to the term "empirical." "Abstract" thus comes to mean *nonempirical°*, and, presumably, the more abstract a proposition, the more nonempirical it is. Surely, however, if ever there were a binary distinction, it is that between empirical and nonempirical. Albert Einstein's famous equation, $e = mc^2$, is as abstract as one can get in the field of physics—it applies supposedly to all material phenomena—but it is certainly not a nonempirical statement. It is *mathematically stated°*, but it is not a mathematical statement. The equation is every bit as empirical as, for instance, the generalization that the offspring of a jenny and a horse or of a donkey and a mare are sterile. Most of the general propositions in this volume are on the highest level of abstraction relative to the term "society"—that is, they refer to any and all societies. Each and every one of them is, nevertheless, empirical. Whether any *concrete social system°* called a society will, or does, have family systems as some of its subsystems is an empirical question. All such propositions are, at least in theory, subject to empirical disproof, although not to final proof. After all, to get final proof for such a proposition, one would have to be able to examine all known and unknown societies past and present and all societies in the future.

The greatest sin committed in this study is not that the most general propositions on which all the others rest are stated as axioms, or that quite abstract, highly generalized implications are derived from those axioms. Rather, it is that all of these propositions are presented as "hypotheses about the facts," as it were, without any attempt to marshal even the extant materials on families, mothers, infants, fathers, and so forth. Each of these hypotheses is carefully stated so that, conceivably, each is falsifiable. I take no refuge in evasion, such as saying: "Most societies to some extent, given ordinary circumstances, have families as subsystems." I flatly state that all known societies have family subsystems. None of these propositions—neither the ones presented as axioms nor the ones taken as implications of those axioms—has been "proved." Nevertheless, each is phrased so that even a single exception would cast doubt on it. If evidence can be found of a single entity called a society without family subsystems, it would seriously detract from the relevance of this work, even though such evidence might not have far-reaching implications for the vast majority of societies past and present.

I have tried to take a small number of very abstract propositions to see something of where they lead. Those propositions and their implications are stated with as few qualifications as possible, not to pass them off as proved but, rather, to make the exceptions emerge as clearly as possible.

A scientist does not expect his or her propositions to be correct forever, but seeks to phrase propositions only in order to learn as much as possible from either their verification or their disproof. Identify a society that lacks the kind of asymmetry asserted by Axiom V and practically every other proposition of this work is called into question. That society, however, will raise an entirely new set of extremely interesting questions. How is initial socialization carried out there? What behaviors are still held in common by members of this society and members of others? The most extreme implication of such a hypothetical finding would be that the initial socialization of infants could produce results that varied at random to the inculcator of that socialization. Such a finding would with high probability, if not certainty, constitute at least an initial step toward biological reduction of the behavior of infants.

Even though none of the elements called "social" here is an elegant biological reduction, the social is not treated as nonbiological but, rather, as a specific subcategory of the biological that is not yet explicable in terms of two of the most general biological concepts, human heredity and the nonhuman environment. Everything not elegantly reduced to biology (or not puristically biological) is considered social, but it is not regarded as impervious to such reduction. The social, as it is used in this volume, is not nonbiological. It is not nonphysical either, any more than the biological is nonphysical. Accordingly, I reject all mind-body distinctions as mystical rather than scientific. That may be sinning, but it is metascientific, not scientific, sinning.

Another of the more fundamental sins of this volume is that it contains virtually no references to developmental psychology. Quite apart from my inexpertise in this area, which will be obvious to any reader, there is another reason for the omission. I have tried to focus attention on the level of any human society, and little, if any, of the literature of developmental psychology has made any special attempt to allow for such a level of generality, even hypothetically.

There is another reason for this neglect. The focus of my interest here is on some implications of extremely general patterns of social interaction as observed in the first three, four, or five years of life. Specifically, my focus is on the asymmetry of maternal attention as compared with paternal attention. Thus, it makes little difference to this argument whether the ability to speak generally emerges in the ninth month or the sixth month, or whether it emerges only after the infant has acquired a certain level of control over his or her eye muscles, facial gestures, and so forth.

What does make a difference in this study is who has been interacting with that infant when he or she acquires a command of speech, insofar as social interaction is relevant to such mastery. If the nature of that person is irrelevant to the infant's command of language, then it is irrelevant to the discussion attempted here. In other words, I do not venture very far into developmental psychology. I ask what certain very abstract propositions imply about the individuals involved. All I attempt is to observe that a mother's role is preponderantly influential in this social-

ization of infants and young children. I do not attempt—
and that may be another major sin of this work—to speculate about the further implications, if any, of this asymmetry. Practically the only things stated along this line of
"further implications" are, first, that initial socialization is
not likely to vary at random to an individual's later development, and, second, that the source of that initial socialization *is* overwhelmingly likely to be female. What
would make an enormous difference for both developmental theory and this work would be a finding, for example, that infants reared asymmetrically by males learn
to talk at, say, the age of five months or twenty-five
months, whereas those reared asymmetrically by women
learn at fifteen months.

This book does not discuss whether learning, and the
subsequent influence of that learning, is autonomic. The
hypothesis is simply stated that a great deal of learning is
social and hence, by definition, nonautonomic, given our
present level of knowledge. I doubt an infant would learn
to walk if no other human intervened or attempted to
teach the infant. I am much more confident, however,
that an infant would not learn to walk in a socially expected or accepted fashion without the intervention of
some other human, almost certainly the mother.

We are told that peristalsis in kittens will not occur unless the mother cat stimulates her kittens' bellies with as-
siduous licking. If so, peristalsis itself is not autonomic in
kittens even if it can also be shown that such maternal intervention is itself autonomic. Because the social is always part of the biological, it would not be surprising to
find elegant biological reductions of many of the phenomena presently considered social. The challenge for sociobiologists is to produce them. What would be surprising and what would invalidate the line of country taken
here would be the discovery that the mothers' relevance
to socialization is trivial or nonexistent.

Jerome Bruner, in a personal letter, has raised a critical and relevant series of questions about this work. He asks why I consider the first encounter, the first occasion on which something is done or learned, the first who teaches us, to be *the* crucial one. My response is that I would not regard any of those "firsts" as *the* crucial one. Such a judgment depends on one's criteria of "*the* crucial." Each of those "firsts" is almost certainly—I am prepared to be deterministic about it—*is* certainly *a* crucial one. This initial learning is crucial at least in the sense that either subsequent learning is based on it or that it must be unlearned before a new base can replace it. I suspect that no subsequent learning is ever totally dissociated from initial learning, although as one ages and stores a great deal in his or her memory, the relationship may become attenuated. It is not likely to be something of which one is consciously aware.

From shortly after birth on, certainly there is no *tabula rasa*°! I doubt it makes much difference in the long run whether one stores the concept "milk" in *memory*° before storing the concept "apple." I doubt it affects many things directly. The language we initially store, however, is probably much more relevant to everything we do subsequently. What I maintain here is that (1) one set of circumstances, wherein all initial learning occurs, has not been generally recognized or fully explored; (2) one may legitimately wonder if there are teachers who are ever as important as the first teachers, and, if so, in what respects; and (3) one can make many generalizations about who or what these initial teachers are—generalizations that are neither tautologically true nor trivially false.

I do not hold, as Bruner thinks I do, that "the law of primacy is the one and only most powerful principle in the psychology of socialization" (Jerome Bruner, letter to the author, September 1986). I would hold, however, that *it is certainly one of the most powerful;* again, I am not aware of its having received sufficient attention. In most sociological treatments, initial socialization is generally taken for granted and left undiscussed.

The question may be raised that even if initial socialization takes the form discussed here, do we not spend much of our lives having forgotten all about that? Is not infantile amnesia, as it were, a common feature of the species? No one can even plausibly claim to remember the details of how he or she learned to walk, talk, control bodily functions, eat, sleep, or to be male or female in a socially acceptable fashion. Yet, everyone capable of learning such things has done so unless left almost totally neglected. There is a world of difference, however, between the fact that adults rarely, if ever, remember these early lessons with any clarity—though many have been led to think they do—and the proposition that those experiences, so generally out of mind, are effectively without significance. Each of us may learn to be independent of his or her mother. But it is significant that we have to learn such independence. Learning independence, moreover, does not negate the significance of what she has taught us.

As Bruner has observed, rites of passage can be viewed as doing everything possible to reinforce "the shedding of earlier ways and to drive a wedge between a young boy and his maternal tutor" (letter to the author, September 1986). But no one ever completely sheds earlier ways, and no matter how one tries to drive that wedge, mothers are, everywhere and always, a more fundamental influence in our lives than most of us have ever realized. We certainly do not shed their early influence in the sense that a snake sheds its skin and frees itself of that particular bit of epidermis forever.

Is the learning that follows initial socialization essentially superficial—that is, in comparison with what is laid down during that early period? I don't think so at all. But

later learning is based in important respects on initial socialization, whether we like it or not. Freud is not at all
the kind of intellectual figure that Newton is, but he is
undoubtedly every bit as great. One of the most important things about Freud is that, regardless of the substantive errors to be found in his work, the extent to which
he forced our attention back to the "primal" stages is
difficult to gainsay. Some say he overdid it, and some
even say he got it all wrong. I hope not to overdo maternal asymmetry and its influence on early socialization in
this book but, rather, to place emphasis on a general
characteristic of that early stage everywhere—on the universal asymmetry of maternal care.

The fact that child abusers have so often been abused as
children themselves reminds me of the Old Testament
warning about "visiting the sins of the fathers upon the
children." When I contemplate the importance of these
earlier influences, my sense of humor tells me that my
emphasis on maternal influence over initial socialization
has nothing to do with a romantic fascination with what
comes first or with psychoanalysis. It is, rather, Jesuitical.
After all, it was the Jesuits who are reported to have said:
"Give us a child till the age of five, and you can have him
after that." Maybe they said "six."

Bruner has also asked why I give "such a powerful
place to the *sources* of our representations of the world
and of ourselves" (letter to the author, September 1986).
My reply is that the "power" those sources hold for our
future has not received sufficient attention. Some of the
universalities about the *setting*° for those sources have, on
the whole, especially escaped notice. We are all of us familiar with the adage that "the hand that rocks the cradle
is the hand that rules the world," but we certainly have
not investigated the meaning of such common sense.

We have tended on the whole to believe that one
should render unto men the things that are male and unto

women the things that are female. But, if anything, the
concepts of power and the superego have overbalanced us
in the direction of the male. When Freud spoke of the superego, it had universal resonance in social history. For
all societies, political precedence has, in the last analysis,
been taken by males, at least ideally speaking, and, for
the most part, actually as well. Mothers, however, have
played a bigger role even in male precedence than we
credit them. It is mothers who first teach us of male
precedence. Thus, I would not give initial maternal
influences *all* the weight. I nevertheless believe much
more attention should be given to how the subsequent
influences enter in and overbear these origins—when and
if that happens.

Some may raise the question of "discontinuities" in the
growth of the mind. I am not sure I know what is meant
by "discontinuities." In sloppy hands, they can become
"immanent" or "emergent" properties with inexplicable
origins. One can use discontinuities in another sense,
however, which is far more respectable scientifically. But
such discontinuities need to be rather clearly explicated—
for instance, the freedom of the discontinuities from the
continuities, and the source and nature of that freedom.
In order to discuss discontinuities in a nonmystical sense,
one cannot grant the *continuities* a monopolistic importance not because this would involve a "totally empiristic
learning theory" (Bruner, letter to the author, September
1986), but because one suspects it would be empirically
false and misleading.

By my carrying everything back and stressing the
influence of mothers, some will feel that the question of
economic allocation has been reduced to an absurdity. It
is interesting that the question of similarly reducing political allocation is not as likely to be raised. Most people do
not like to think of breast-feeding as economic allocation,
though they readily see a slap as an exercise of power.

Under modern conditions, we tend to regard economic allocation as overwhelmingly specialized in nonfamily contexts, which of course it never is. Worse, we tend to think economic allocation somehow does not enter one's life until one reaches a certain level of what might be called *allocative puberty°*. Just as sexuality does not begin with puberty, so economic allocation does not wait until near-adulthood to develop.

Many individuals may worry that I have neglected the "stages" of development in this book. Although many "stage" theories seem to me nonsensical or even meretricious, I respect the work of people like Jean Piaget and Maria Montessori, and I would not want to rule out such theories. But I am not convinced that these theories are scientifically fruitful here. What I cannot imagine, however, is any stage theory that rules out the relevance of the initial stages or that is based on a sort of tabula-rasa assumption to the effect that, with regard to, say, stage six, nothing that happened before need be relevant.

I have certainly sinned in not even trying to divide infancy and early childhood into any further stages. Part of that omission is sheer lack of expertise. I have even sinned more on that score because the beginning of the period I discuss is birth (completely omitting any discussion of prenatal influence), but the other end is left rather open-ended. It is never defined here more tightly than "three, four, or five years of age." If challenged, I suppose I would accept that the end of this early period is as early as the age of three. What I have done, without going into it in any detail, is simply to take that period of life during which the mother's role is everywhere highly asymmetrical in the respects I discuss. I understand that the distinction between infancy and early childhood is of some importance, but the main point is that this period of time is highly relevant to virtually all that follows. One may, of course, trivialize the theory of stages, which may be done by observing that one must learn to walk before one can learn to run. But is even this observation trivial? Particularly with regard to later age distinctions, developmental theory spends little time discussing the relevance of what comes earlier. Here again, we certainly owe it to Freud to be more careful.

I have also not taken into consideration a kind of instant "unassisted" learning, nor have I even scouted the extent to which such learning rests on the initial socialization that I discuss. This learning may be best described in an adaptation of Mark Twain's observation (1897), paraphrased here, that when a cat sits on a red-hot stove lid, that cat will move, and that cat will never sit on another red-hot stove lid, but it will never sit on another cold one either.[1] All would agree, without much quibbling, that such learning rests little, if at all, on what is "mother-taught." Here, the lesson itself is its own reinforcement and, as such, is relevant to a very small amount of the variance or of the underlying commonalities of human behavior. If that hypothesis is incorrect, then what is written here will have little relevance to such learning and vice versa.

Many will also ask about the time the father spends with the child. Isn't it crucial for the inculcations discussed? If the allocation of time is as asymmetrical as I allege, then one has to make some special assumptions that father-time somehow constitutes special "quality time." That is a far-fetched notion. Nothing but universally held traditional beliefs about the importance of fathers supports this hypothesis.

There is another problem in this regard. Father-time varies along two dimensions at least. First, by contrast

1. What Twain actually says is: "We should be careful to get out of experience only the wisdom that is in it—and stop there; lest we be like the cat that sits on a hot stove-lid. She will never sit down on a hot stove-lid again—and that is well; but also she will never sit down on a cold one any more" (1897, p. 125).

with the time spent by a mother, the time a father actually spends *even in the presence of* an infant or young child is highly variable depending on what the father does (some go off to fish for weeks at a time). Second, even when a father is at home, he spends far less time interacting with an infant or young child than does the mother. How and to what extent he interacts when he is present are both much more highly variable for him than for the mother. Therefore, generalization about *all* fathers is more difficult. One thing that can be generalized about the father's role is that his frequent presence enables the infant or young child to observe his or her father, thus providing a basis for validating or otherwise affecting the child's interpretation of the mother's account of what males are like.

In addition, it would seem especially clear that the presence or attention of fathers is neither frequent nor constant enough to establish patterns either of masculinity in male offspring or stereotypes about males for female offspring. *These patterns are established for the infant or young child by the mother, who is, in an interesting sense, the primary* role model° *for her male offspring as well as for her female ones.* She is a male role model and a female role model. When the mother is establishing these patterns in her male offspring, she alters her voice and gestures to assume or imitate male patterns. The presence of a father or another male could well validate or otherwise affect, through an offspring's own observations, what the infant or child stores in her or his memory about such matters.

Many behaviors are not learned until much later in life. Literacy is one of these. Bearing a child may be another, if one is female, though many females aged five or younger have borne close witness to a mother's childbearing. Fathering an infant is another. None of these is, of course, precisely prefigured by the early socialization discussed here, but certainly none of these varies at random to that socialization.

I have not speculated about the future, though perhaps I should. What if we reverse this asymmetry and find that it makes no difference whether mothers or fathers have the preponderantly influential relationship with offspring? What if it makes no difference in the rearing of either male or female offspring? Such findings would argue that sex differentiation of adults who care for children is irrelevant to the socialization of offspring, and if this held for the sex differentiation of the offspring, too, one would be almost completely driven back on an as yet unexplained puristically biological determinism. Within our time there may be some elegant biological reductions, but these are not likely to render sex differentiation irrelevant either to the rearing of offspring or to the development of the offspring themselves.

For a social explanation, one would be compelled to emphasize that the individual interacting with the offspring is overwhelmingly likely to be an adult. Attention would be shifted to a hypothesis, undoubtedly true (but not nearly so likely to be fruitful), that the initial socialization of human beings is overwhelmingly likely to be inculcated on offspring by adults.

If sex-role differentiation should prove irrelevant to the socialization of offspring, then emphasis on absolute-age role differentiation (in this case, adulthood) is not likely to be fruitful. Rather, one would probably be forced to seek more puristically biological explanations *without* there being any elegant biological reductions in hand. Far from requiring the sociobiologist to put up or shut up, that rather forfeits the game.

Finally, I have not supported this work with any of the customary bibliographical paraphernalia. What, for example, of Johann J. Bachofen's book, *Das Mutterrecht* (1861)? My command of German is not in nearly good enough repair for me to have read the book carefully, but from such knowledge as I glean from other sources, it says little that is relevant to my present line of argument.

Indeed, Bachofen posits an early *matriarchy*°, a view almost totally repudiated by social scientists today.[2] Similarly, Edward Westermarck's epic work, *The History of
Human Marriage* (1891), is, alas, not on the subject treated
here, although he has much to say that sociobiologists
might wish to study.

Recently, there has been an enormously increased interest in the roles women play today, have played in the
past, and might play in the future. Much of this literature
focuses on the authors' normative concerns, but it has
nevertheless significantly increased our understanding of
both history and the present.

One looks in vain, however, for a study on the subject
of this book. When I first learned of a volume by Nancy
Chodorow (1978) generally called *Mothering,* I started to
put away my materials. I assumed Chodorow had done
what I was setting out to do. When her book came into
my hands, however, I found that its title was in fact *The
Reproduction of Mothering: Psychoanalysis and the Sociology
of Gender* and that her main preoccupation was along a
quite different line. The second section in part I of her
book states the major problem clearly: "Why women
mother." Any reader of her work will be quick to note,
however, that she articulates the nub of my preoccupation in the first paragraph of her introduction. I quote it
in its entirety. It is very good.

> Women mother. In our society, as in most societies,
> women not only bear the children, they also take primary

2. This position was repudiated on the basis of careful studies published more than a quarter of a century ago in a volume entitled *Matrilineal Kinship,* David M. Schneider and Kathleen Gough, editors
(1961). The book begins by noting that it appeared "just 100 years after the publication of Johann J. Bachofen's *Das Mutterrecht,* which first
posed matrilineal descent as a problem." Unless they, and practically
every other source I have been able to find that mentions Bachofen,
have misstated what he was about, he was not about what is under-
taken here.

responsibility for infant care, spend more time with infants than do men, and sustain primary emotional ties
with infants. When biological mothers do not parent,
other women, rather than men, virtually always take their
place. Though fathers and other men spend varying
amounts of time with infants and children, the father is
rarely a child's primary parent. (p. 3)

I did not get the idea from Chodorow, though I certainly might have had I seen her book early enough, just
as I might have gotten it from the Reverend William Law
(see the epigraph to this book) as early as 1762. I was well
into this volume before I read her book in 1984. When I
read that paragraph, I thought nothing was left to do.
But at the end of that very same page, Chodorow made it
quite clear that she was after different, and perhaps much
bigger, game. She states: "This book analyzes women's
mothering, and, in particular, the way women's mothering is reproduced across generations. Its central question
is how do women today come to mother? By implication it asks how we might change things to transform
the sexual division of labor in which women mother"
(pp. 3–4). From there on our interests diverge.

As I said in the preface, I came even later to Dorothy
Dinnerstein's book, *The Mermaid and the Minotaur: Sexual
Arrangements and Human Malaise* (1976) (see p. xvi). She is
concerned with the asymmetrical role of women in infant
and child care. She and Chodorow, however, share an
agendum that I do not possess. That agendum appears in
the subtitle of Dinnerstein's book, "Sexual Arrangements
and Human Malaise." They wish to fix things. They are
certainly interested in truth, I think, but not so much in
science. Often, when I agree with them, I find I cannot
put what is said on a generalized parsimonious, scientific
basis. Perhaps much of it *could* be put on such a basis.

I still find it hard to credit that so obvious a bit of the
puzzle of human explanation as the asymmetry of mater-

nal care for infants and young children can have been so
generally overlooked or, when noted, not studied systematically. After all, the Reverend Law had the nub of
this idea as early as 1762, Dinnerstein had it in 1976, and
Chodorow had it in 1978. Hundreds of quotations might
be assembled from the intervening two centuries, and
myriads more might be culled from the centuries before.
Nevertheless, I know of no attempt to explore, systematically and scientifically, this alleged asymmetry of human
existence. This book is only a first step in that direction.

As noted above, the greatest sin of this work is not that
it is nonempirical or purely deductive or anything of that
sort. It is, rather, that the empirical content is presented
as a matter of speculation, as hypotheses about the facts,
or as axioms, rather than as the detailed marshaling of
data, which I regard as inadequate, in any event, to
confirm finally my hypotheses. In addition, I am unaware
of any data that contradict any of my propositions as
stated. All of these propositions are, however, falsifiable
empirically, as I have stated earlier.

There is one sin I have not committed, but in not com-
mitting it I may well have sinned in another manner. I
have not built evaluations into this analysis. The propositions here are about all peoples' normative patterns, but
the propositions are not normative in and of themselves. I
do not say anything about whether this asymmetry is
good, bad, or indifferent. All I say about asymmetry, I
say in a social setting that is emotionally charged. Therefore, I may well have sinned by not continually iterating
that I am engaged not in evaluation but, rather, in specu-
lating about what is.

There is another closely associated set of scientific sins
that I have *not* committed here. I have not said that this
state of affairs will continue indefinitely, although I think
it will. I have certainly not said that the present situation
ought to be perpetuated. We presently possess no knowledge that would enable us to predict that human beings

could not, if they wished to do so, alter maternal asymmetry in the care and supervision of infants and young
children. I doubt we will substantially alter things, but
my saying so does not render it impossible. One may
also speculate as to whether we can, in fact, rear viable
human beings using alternative patterns. That question
can be discussed in a nonnormative fashion as well,
though not without reference to the normative patterns
of the people concerned. Two questions are eminently interesting from both a scientific and a normative point of
view: First, can our mother-tempers be replaced by un-
differentiated parent-tempers or father-tempers or yet-
unimagined tempers? Second, if they can be, will they
be? There is, I suppose, yet a third question after those
two: If our tempers cease to be our mother-tempers,
what will our tempers be?

4

The Family

For the present, the most general key to generalities about human beings lies in the analysis of family structure. It is therefore meet to begin with a definition of *kinship structures*° in general; of the family in particular; and, by residual definition, of all other social structures. Kinship structures (patterns) are defined here as that portion of a society for which, in addition to other orientations, sometimes equally, if not more important, the membership of the unit(s) concerned and the nature of the solidarity among the *members*° are, to some extent at least, determined by orientation to the facts of biological relatedness (descent) and/or *sexual intercourse*°. (N.B.: One may, of course, wish to distinguish between legitimate and illegitimate, between institutionalized and noninstitutionalized, kinship structures.) But nonkinship social structures such as *some,* but never all, geographical, political, economic, religious, etc., structures are never of negligible importance. For many purposes of analysis—depending on the society and the problem posed—nonkinship social structures may be a great deal more relevant than kinship structures. Moreover, for all societies prior to what may be called modernized societies today, relatively few social structures contained no kinship elements whatsoever. Even those that, ideally, contain no kinship elements do not vary at random to kinship structures, even in the context of *high modernization*°.

All *membership units°* of all societies may be divided into four categories. Three of those four are *kinship units°*: (1) *descent units°,* that is, *organizations°* or relationships, membership for which is oriented at least in part to biological relatedness (via descent); (2) *sexual-intercourse units°,* membership for which is oriented at least in part to sexual intercourse but not to biological relatedness (via descent); and (3) *family units°,* that is, kinship units for which membership is oriented at least in part to *biological descent°* and to sexual intercourse. All other membership units are (4) *nonkinship units°*—that is to say, they are *concrete structures°* (or membership units), inclusion in which is oriented to neither biological descent nor sexual intercourse. Among kinship units, descent units are overwhelmingly more relevant to general social organization than are sexual-intercourse units. And of the four categories, family units are overwhelmingly more relevant than any other unit(s) for any general explanations of social phenomena. The far-reaching social relevance of family units is almost a truism.

First there is no known society, past or present, without family patterns (see Axiom I, p. 18). Indeed, there are no social systems whose members have not experienced some behavior in family contexts. The only other organizational context about whose universal presence one may be similarly confident is the interdependence among members of two or more different family units—some form, however rudimentary, of government—and action in terms of governments affects infants and young children in few if any ways directly perceived by them. Another true, but not trivial, observation (see Axiom II, p. 18) along these lines is that in all known societies infants are born into some sort of family context. Initial social placement of all infants is in some sense a function of family placement.

Whatever the complexities of the learning curve for human individuals, the initial part of that curve—and hence the part on which all subsequent learning is based—is from birth to age three, four, or five (see Axiom III, p. 19). For the overwhelming proportion of humankind, past and even present, the initial learning curve is experienced primarily in a family context. It is in a family context that the overwhelming majority of all human beings, past, present, and presumably future, learn to walk, to talk, to eat, to sleep, to control bodily functions and to interact with other human beings. It is in a family context that one becomes a social being. These generalizations hold for Lapps and Lithuanians, for Greeks and Jews, for Buddhists and the followers of Islam, for Chinese and Burmese, for Trobriand Islanders and Iroquois—for all peoples of any place or any time.

In the contexts of all known societies from birth to death, *absolute age°* distinctions, however complicated, cover four categories in some more or less complex way. Those four categories are infancy, childhood, *adulthood°*, and *old age°*. For all known societies, with rare exceptions, every individual at every stage of her or his life cycle is identifiable as a member of one or more family units. *From birth to death, human beings are "family beings,"* however attenuated that family connection may become in some social settings at some times.

All nonkinship units, indeed all *nonfamily units°*, may be divided into two categories: First, for *nonfamily units of Type I°* family considerations ideally affect one's behavior in a nonfamily context. For example, in imperial China how one behaved in the context of one's village was ideally *and* actually based largely on how such actions might affect one's family and family members. Second, for *nonfamily units of Type II°*—rather rare until the past 150 years—ideally, family considerations do not affect an individual's behavior in the nonfamily context concerned. For example, how a university professor deals with a student is ideally not affected by family or other kinship considerations.

In the context of Type I units, ideally speaking, family experiences are supposed to affect one's behavior. It is overwhelmingly probable that one's actual behavior in nonfamily contexts will in fact be affected by family experiences. It is also overwhelmingly probable, however, that even in the context of Type II nonfamily units, for which family expectations are not considered relevant, family experiences will affect one's actual behavior.

The family is the only known unit (or social organization) common to all human beings for which the ordinary expectation is that, at all stages of an individual's life, she or he will (1) belong to some family unit and that (2) family experiences ideally and/or actually will affect his or her behavior in every other social context. This is most obviously an implication of Axiom III regarding the initial part of everyone's learning curve, on which all subsequent learning is based. Such learning falls largely, if not overwhelmingly, into a family context for all people. The relevance of this experience for other contexts, however, is always and everywhere a function of other elements as well.[1]

It may also be generalized that, regardless of social conditions in some parts of the world over the past two centuries, nearly all individuals have spent more time in family contexts than in any other social context. But if one separates out these relatively modernized contexts, an even stronger statement can be made: Prior to the nineteenth century, nearly all people regardless of geography or chronology (probably well in excess of 85 percent of them) spent the overwhelming majority of their lives (probably well in excess of 85 percent of their lives) within eyeshot and/or earshot of some other member(s)

---

1. For example, the family is overwhelmingly likely to be a major focus, if not *the* major focus, of role differentiation, solidarity, economic allocation, political allocation, and integration and expression throughout the life cycle.

of their own families.[2] In addition, some societies—by no means all—have been characterized by *institutions*° that prescribe that individuals give priority to family considerations over any and all other considerations. The above claims or hypotheses will not hold true, even in close approximation of the truth, for any nonfamily unit discerned in human history. Such far-reaching relevance and influence can be claimed only for families.

The initial inculcation of family patterns on infants and very young children is always and everywhere ideally and/or actually carried out by mothers.

2. The 85 percent figure has been chosen somewhat arbitrarily. I think it is not too high. It may be too low. Even when some members of a society go on hunting, fishing, or military expeditions, those who go almost never constitute anything approaching a majority of the total membership; they almost never go alone, and some one or more of those who accompany them are likely to be family members.

5

Role Differentiation

Every society has specifically differentiated patterns of who does what when, that is, role differentiation. The patterns most relevant here are made on the basis of *age°, generation°*, sex, economic allocation, and political allocation. The first three are treated together here, and discussions of economic and political role differentiations appear in separate sections of this chapter.

AGE, GENERATION, AND SEX DIFFERENTIATION

Of the varying forms of role differentiation characteristic of all known societies, three—age, generation, and sex—have underlain all the others. That is, infants and young children initially learn all role differentiations other than these three types as one or some combination of the three. Role differentiation on the basis of age is always further broken down on the bases of absolute age and *relative age°*. Role differentiation on the basis of generation is always, as a minimum, broken down into a distinction between *older* and *younger* generations. Role differentiation on the basis of sex for all known societies is broken down, as a minimum, into the categories of *male* and *female*.

In all social phenomena one may distinguish between *basic* and *specialized* characteristics. Some role differentiations that are characteristic of all societies—such as differentiations on the bases of infancy, childhood, adulthood, and old age, younger and older, and younger generation and older generation—are always basic distinctions. All members of all societies are originally regarded as infants and subsequently as children, adults, and aged (or whatever absolute-age distinctions are institutionalized for the society), if they survive long enough. These are absolute-age distinctions. Everyone is regarded as chronologically older or younger than someone else. These are relative-age distinctions. All are also regarded as representatives of earlier ("older") or later ("younger") generations depending on their relation(s) to other individuals.

But there is no basic form of sex-role differentiation. All sex roles are specialized. For all known societies, the treatment of infants from birth varies as a function of whether they are classified as male or female by those who interact with them. Role differentiation on the basis of sex may therefore be regarded as the first learned form of variance, or specialization. It is the first learning of a specialization that is characteristic of that individual but not of all of the members of the society. Approximately 50 percent of every population learn they are specialized as male and 50 percent as female. This initial learning of variance, or specialization, takes place in nearly all human cases in a family context (see Axiom IV, pp. 19–20).

As stated above, role differentiation on the bases of age, generation, and sex underlies all other role differentiations. For all known societies, for example, roles are also differentiated on the bases of economic allocation, political allocation, *religion°, cognition°,* the nonhuman environment, solidarity, and stratification as a minimum. All of these in all known societies are originally taught and learned in a family context in terms of distinctions based on age, generation, and sex. One may learn, for example, that one is a "follower" because one is a child, or a member of a younger generation, or a female, or some combination of the set. One does not learn that one is a child or a younger-generation person or a female because one is a follower. Nearly all human beings not only learn to walk, talk, sleep, eat, control bodily functions, and interact with other human beings in a family context, but also to view these things initially as aspects associated with age, generation, and sex. Moreover, in the case of sex-role differentiation, they learn they differ, in ways that will never be bridged, from approximately 50 percent of their own and every other age *cohort°*. Finally, however banal it may seem to state it explicitly, this family-based learning is the foundation on which all subsequent learning is somehow superimposed, whether in family contexts or not. This learning is everywhere and at all times initially received from one's mother.

For those 85+ percent of all human beings who in the past at least (i.e., prior to modernization) spent 85+ percent of all of their lives within eyeshot and/or earshot of other members of their own families, one would expect on the basis of chronology alone that most economic and political allocations, and behavior that is religiously oriented or stratified, and so forth, would take place in family contexts. *But even in more modernized contexts, the largest proportion of all role differentiation continues to take place in a family context,* where—arguably over the life cycle—individuals may not spend more than, say, 35 percent of their waking and sleeping hours within eyeshot and/or earshot of some other member of their own family.

Even under highly modernized conditions, the family context remains enormously important in all these respects, if only because one is likely to spend more time there than in any other single organizational context. For all members of all societies this generalization holds, or at least holds for all societies and the overwhelming majority of their members. It holds asymmetrically for females, who even in nonmodern contexts probably spend more time in family contexts than do males. *It holds, however, much more asymmetrically for women in modernized contexts.* In all such contexts so far, including those of *latecomers°* to modernization, females spend a much higher proportion of their time in family contexts than do males.

A specific artifact of recent social history is that many regard economic and political aspects of life as taking place outside the family. Most human beings for most of history have certainly not thought so. Indeed, for the majority of human beings, even in the present time, that is almost certainly not the case. Prior to modernization, the family was the major context of economic and political allocation for most of the people most of the time.

Back of the development in the nineteenth century of the first relatively modernized societies lies the great reservoir of human variance. Whether people like it or not, as societies move in the direction of modernization, they converge in more and more respects. In relatively modernized societies *multilineal conjugal families°* become the norm. *Families of orientation°* and *families of procreation°* tend to differ for males and females. Families are predominantly *patriarchal°* on both sides of the modernization dividing line, but *patrilineality°* is replaced by *multilineality°* rather than *matrilineality°*, and *patrilocality°* and *matrilocality°* are both replaced by *neolocality°*, and so forth. It is on the nonmodernized side of the line—that is, where most human experience resides—that the great variance in kinship and family structures, at least in their ideal pattens, if not so much in their actual patterns, is shown in its full colors. It is here that one finds *extended families°, stem families°,* and *conjugal (nuclear) families°,* in addition to the widest variety of marital selection systems, the broadest variance in sexual practices, and the like. At least, that variance is present as far as the ideal patterns are concerned.

Actually, even here, the picture is much less varied for most people most of the time. Throughout most of his-

tory very high rates of infant mortality and otherwise relatively short life-expectancies render the following observations roughly true. Despite preferences for large
families and the like, the average number of members per
family unit has probably never much exceeded four or, at
most, five. Of these four or five family members, the
probability has been overwhelming that only two generations were in fact represented at any given time; indeed,
the average may not be as high as two. High infant mortality meant that very few more than two siblings per
marital pair survived to maturity. Very few more than
two generations are long represented in any single family.
Some family units must consist of parents whose children
are no longer with them, married couples who have not
yet had children, and so forth. Because the sex ratio at
birth is roughly one to one, 50 percent of the families will
have two male and two female members; 25 percent will
have one male and three female members; and 25 percent
will have one female and three male members. Two family members will be older-generation members, and two
will belong to the younger generation (see Coale et al.,
1965, esp. pp. 40–69). Probably the greatest form of variance leading to increased members for any given family
would not have increased the number of generations represented but, rather, the number of nonadult siblings
alive at any given time.[1]

The membership of most family units has therefore
consisted of someone identified as a father, a mother
(who, of course, could be more reliably identified than
the father), one son and one daughter, or two daughters,
or two sons, the children being either infants or young
children. Under nonmodernized conditions the family of
procreation is likely to be a continuation of the family
of orientation for either the husband or the wife.

1. This is highly conjectural even for me. I am not in any way
qualified as a demographer.

When one crosses over the line into relatively modernized conditions, the actual picture remains much the same because, among other changes, the ideal patterns change in the direction of multilineal conjugal patterns. Here the average number of membership of the family unit is less than four, and the generations presented do not average out to as many as two. If the unit has four members, two generations are likely to be represented by two males and two females, two older-generation representatives, two younger-generation representatives, and so forth. Insofar as role differentiation on the bases of age, generation, and sex has much to do with human beings learning to walk, to talk, to eat, to sleep, to control bodily functions, to behave as females and males, and to interact with other human beings, *the units in terms of which human beings have experienced the initial part of their learning curves, on which all else is in some sense based, have varied remarkably little through time and space.* However little they may have varied in other respects, the asymmetrical role of the mother in child-rearing has varied even less.

Ethical and moral preferences notwithstanding, the family has always been a *hierarchical°* organization. Ideally, precedence, at least prior to retirement, is taken by older absolute-age representatives over younger ones, by relatively older people over relatively younger ones, by representatives of older generations over representatives of younger ones, and by males over females. Those hierarchies come in varying combinations, to be sure, but in general they characterize all family systems for all societies.[2] In family contexts not only has the allocation of *power°* and *responsibility°* followed such lines, but so too has the allocation of goods and services.

---

2. Ordinarily these different bases tend to reinforce one another (see below, pp. 54–55). It should also be noted, however, that a relatively younger, even an absolutely younger, male may, ideally speaking, succeed as family head if he is of an older generation.

In the context of all known societies, all infants and young children learn some socially expected and accepted forms of behavior on the bases of absolute and relative age, younger and older generations, and sex. They have specifically learned about precedence on these bases. All of these behaviors and social expectations as they apply to themselves are initially learned via interaction with their respective mothers. Initial role differentiations on the bases of age, generation, and sex are mother-taught.

ECONOMIC ROLE DIFFERENTIATION:
PRODUCTION ROLES AND CONSUMPTION ROLES

Production roles° and *consumption roles°* are always differentiated on the bases of absolute age, relative age, generation, and sex. *These variances never vary at random to either the allocations of power and responsibility or the general hierarchy of the family context.*

For nearly all human beings—regardless of variations in time, place, culture, and so forth—the family has been the social context in terms of which nearly all economic allocation has taken place. Before modernization the distinction between production and consumption lacked the concrete implications it has today. Even for most *moderns°*, of course, production from one point of view *is* consumption from another. But the view that "productive" activities can be carried on largely outside a family context for most people is a quite recent, bizarre development and continued to be a relative rarity long after factories began to develop. After all, it was not until the turn of the century that the overwhelming majority of any population lived or worked outside of rural or nomadic contexts. The Venetian city-states and the Hanseatic League may have constituted exceptions to this rule, but only because they developed extensive, symbiotic relations with predominantly agrarian peoples.

In all premodern contexts the family was the organizational locus for nearly all economic allocation. Also, distinctions between production and consumption were not the focus of concern they later became when development of specialized patterns made it possible (in a vulgar, though not in an *analytic°*, sense) to regard the family as the locus of consumption and factories or offices or the like as the loci of production.

For all nonmodernized societies, regardless of the most widely varying ideal patterns with regard to chastity and the like, female roles in economic allocation are always distinguished from male roles. Even when men and women do similar things, they tend to do them on a sexually segregated basis. Even in our most nearly sexually egalitarian societies today, there is still a great deal of sex-role differentiation in economic allocation. Such differentiations are inculcated on infants and young children by their mothers.

POLITICAL ROLE DIFFERENTIATION

Political allocation—that is, the allocation of power and responsibility—is nearly always observed as an aspect of the family context in nonmodernized, and still importantly to be observed as an aspect of the family context in even the most modernized, societies. As observed earlier, precedence in the family is overwhelmingly determined on the bases of age, generation, and sex; older absolute-age distinctions, or relatively older people, assume precedence over younger ones, and representatives of older generations take precedence over representatives of younger generations. As a rule, males take precedence and have authority over females as well as other younger or younger-generation males. Even matrilineal families have male heads. Women sometimes become family heads by default, owing to the absence of a "properly" qualified male, but they never succeed to family headship by ideal. Ideally speaking, even married sovereigns, if they are female, are not family heads.

Ordinarily these three bases of precedence—age, generation, and sex—reinforce one another. For example, the family head is likely to be the eldest male representative of the eldest generation of the family. But these three things can get out of kilter. It is quite possible for human beings to have a representative of the older generation who is absolutely and, of course, relatively younger than a representative of a younger generation. A representative of the oldest generation present can also be female rather than male.

Various peoples make various compromises when these patterns of precedence do not reinforce one another. In imperial Chinese contexts, for example, generation prevails over age and even over sex in the event of a conflict. In Chinese history a widowed mother, if she were a strong personality, often asserted supremacy not only over the other female members of the family but also over her son and the other males. It was considered wrong, a violation of the ideal patterns, for her, a female, to do this, but it would have been deemed unfilial—an even more unseemly offense—for her son to defy her if she did so assert herself.

What has been said here of political precedence is in no way evaluative. Male precedence in ideal patterns may be considered virtuous or wicked for any reasons that may please one. But this has nothing whatsoever to do with what I allege here. My hypothesis is that male precedence over females in a family context, assuming males have reached maturity, is universally institutionalized in all known societies. That may change, but it has not yet changed generally for any society.

It has been generally stated above that males take precedence in family contexts over females. The form of that precedence, however, varies on many bases. The care and rearing of infants and young children constitutes a significant basis of variation. In all known societies, including even the most modern, the greatest proportion of infant and child care is handled in a family context. Moreover, regardless of the sex of the child, the female side of the family, or *household°*, has far more directly formative roles than does the male side. If, for example, the only older-generation members of the family are a father and a mother, it is the mother who handles the infant, regardless of its sex, for a much greater proportion of time during the formation of the initial part of the infant's learning curve on which all subsequent learning is based. Infants and young children are overwhelmingly reared by older females, regardless of the sex of the offspring. In addition, male infants and female infants are treated differently from birth, regardless of who is dealing with them (see axioms III, IV, and V, pp. 19–20).

Although the father (or perhaps the uncle in matrilineal societies) takes precedence over the mother when there is a conflict of authority, children nevertheless learn about political allocation, economic allocation, and virtually everything else, including how to speak and the like, primarily from older females in the family context. Thus, an older female is more likely than a male to "encourage," "praise," "direct," "give orders," "punish," and "reward" infants and young children, even though the male may do some of these things when he is present. Although fathers may take precedence over mothers, mothers effectively take precedence over fathers with regard to infants and children, teaching them how to behave in terms of power and responsibility, *including how to behave toward their fathers and other males.*

Egalitarianism° in family contexts has not been present even as a *utopian pattern°* for the overwhelming majority of human beings. In recent times, of course, for some of the members of some societies, egalitarianism, especially within family contexts, has become a utopian pattern, if not an actual ideal one. The actual patterns are quite different. However much the types and extent of hierarchy in the family context may vary, there has never been, there is not, and there will never be any such thing as an actual "egalitarian" family. Even if human beings manage—which none have done so far—to abolish all hierarchical distinctions between males and females, such distinctions on generational and age bases will still remain. One may even argue that learning in general does not (even cannot, perhaps) take place on an egalitarian basis. It certainly does not happen that way during the earliest part of the learning curve, that is, from birth to three, four, or five years of age. During those early years the effective hierarchy as far as learning is concerned is that of mothers over offspring.

Both male and female offspring, though treated differently, are largely handled by females up until age five. Prior to modernization, at about age five the males are handled and supervised directly by older males (usually members of the family) and the young females continue to be handled and supervised by older female family members. With modernization, that changes.

Infant and early-childhood education is always importantly focused in a family context—"overwhelmingly focused" would not be putting it too strongly. Until quite recently, this has also been true of most education past that early point of childhood, that is, of education for adulthood. Until the past century or so only small minorities of any population were educated in *school°* contexts. Most education from birth to death for premoderns was conducted within a family context, as was nearly everything else. Even though later childhood education up to adulthood was carried out on a family basis, it was also sexually segregated. This sexual segregation obtained regardless of attitudes toward chastity.

In the past century and a half, people living in modernized contexts have experienced a bizarre development. They have experienced such an emphasis on educationally specialized membership units (i.e., schools) that they ordinarily do not think of education as taking place in the family at all. This holds despite the fact that for moderns, as for everyone else, the earliest part of the learning curve takes place in a family context, even though more and more moderns may utilize day-care and nursery schools at increasingly early ages. Another bizarre development is that school contexts for children from the age of four or five onward are usually *coeducational°*. The extension of the experience of coeducation, either outside or inside a family context, is an extremely recent, highly specialized development in human history.

Clearly for all of those people who spent upward of, say, 85 percent of all of their waking or sleeping hours within eyeshot and/or earshot of their family members, economic and political aspects of life were predominantly focused on a family context—or more properly, conducted within a family context—as were any other aspects or behaviors one cares to distinguish if generalized to a population as a whole. Thus, most actions that could be fruitfully described as predominantly religious or *recreational°*, most emphases on solidarity, and most behavior having to do with integration and expression and the like were largely carried out in a family context.

In relatively modernized contexts, large, ever-increasingly large, amounts of all these behaviors take place in nonfamily, even in nonkinship, contexts. *But even for moderns, more of the set of all such behaviors occurs in a family context than in any other single one.* For the members of all societies, there are always individuals of great significance who are not family members. But the overwhelming proportion of all "significant others"—certainly until the past century and a half, and for most people even now—are members of one's own family.

Great emphasis has been laid here on the relevance of infant and early-childhood education and on economic and political aspects of behavior. Without falling into any narrowly deterministic modes, it is difficult to see how this can be avoided. Infant and early-childhood education is overwhelmingly for all human beings centered in a family context, and that is the foundation on which all subsequent social experience is somehow heaped. If there is a set of people whose children learn to speak almost entirely without reference to a family context, there will be a set of people for whom the family may be virtually irrelevant. No present observers, however, will be able to recognize them readily as human. So far, no one has invented such an alternative.

The political aspects of behavior are emphasized here because human beings are always and everywhere hierarchical in their arrangements. Even when egalitarianism becomes a specific ideal, it is rarely achieved in actuality. If all human beings are in some sense "economic entities," as will be discussed later, they are also "hierarchical entities." At a minimum, none has been able to invent (even if anyone can be said to have sought to do so) child-rearing methods without reference to hierarchical distinctions. All languages make such distinctions. Social contexts in which egalitarianism appears, even as an ideal structure, are on the whole rare.

Friendship° is the only social relationship that can be described as (1) universal—that is, evident in any society—and (2) always ideally egalitarian. One does not have to be either cynical or even knowledgeable about actual friendships to know that, however egalitarian friendships may be ideally, they are rarely devoid of hierarchical aspects in actuality. Despite the universality of friendships, nothing of ongoing significance to the people concerned, other than the value of such relationships to the participants themselves, is ever based on friendship. Friendships are by nature subject to being fractured at the whim of any participant at any time. Long-enduring friendships that survive considerable strain are universally considered unusual.

All human life has required for its continuation some forms of social organization, none of which is carried out on any long-continued basis without differentiations in the allocation of power and responsibility. As we have already observed, the rearing of children, which lies at the very heart of any continuity, always involves such distinctions. Where general records have been kept, the general frame of reference has always involved two factors: chronology and leadership, especially political leadership. There exists a whole set of professionals, historians, whose craft is based on this same frame of reference. Historians must have records to survive, and records, insofar as they have been kept, have been kept largely in terms of chronology and political leadership.

For the earliest social thinkers, the analysis of politics is the most highly developed and sophisticated form of social analysis. This holds true whether one looks to Greek, Chinese, or Hindu philosophy, or whatever. Certainly prior to the mid-eighteenth century, the political analysis of sophisticated thinkers was far more impressive than their economic analysis. After that time, attendant on the exponential increase in the level of generalization of the *media of exchange*° (i.e., *monies*°), the sophistication of economic analysis has far outstripped that of political analysis and has become cumulative.

That is curious. Human beings have always known in some sense that "man does not live by bread alone," but they have also always known that people never live entirely without reference to bread. Whatever one may think of Marx's contribution to humankind in other respects, he made it impossible for us to ignore the fact that, unless only *free goods*° are involved, understanding the allocation of goods and services is strategic in understanding human behavior. Patterns that prove to be nonviable economically will also be nonviable in other respects. Patterns that make economic allocation impossible make human life impossible. It is a problem for social analysis that there is much less insight and attention regarding other aspects of human behavior, aspects that are as "relevant" and "important" as the political and economic ones.

6

Solidarity

For all peoples the family is the multifunctional organizational context par excellence. For most peoples, most role differentiation, solidarity, economic allocation, political allocation, and integration and expression have taken place in family contexts. Even for the most modern peoples more of these role differentiations and so forth take place in family contexts than in any other one. If the family context could be described as predominantly oriented to one of these aspects above all others (but it cannot be so described), it would have to be solidarity. For all peoples the family is the primal context of solidarity. Family interests cut deeper than *class interests°* or any other for most, if not all, individuals—certainly for all peoples. Even when other loyalties take precedence over family loyalties, that precedence is itself a matter of family priorities.

For all human beings the family context is the setting in which patterns of solidarity (and its subcategories, *content°, strength°*, and *intensity°*) are first learned. Although the term "solidarity" is defined technically in the Glossary, it may also be defined more informally as patterns of "who sticks with whom for what purposes and to what relative degree, and how one feels about it." The *content* of solidarity refers to "for what purposes"; the *strength* of solidarity refers to "to what relative degree"; and the *intensity* of solidarity refers to "how one feels about it."

It is important to realize two things from the outset. First, a relationship that is characterized by strong solidarity from one person's point of view may be viewed as weak from another's; for example, a child's relationship with his or her father may take precedence over any other relationship the child has, but the father's relationship with his child may not, and frequently does not, take precedence over the father's relationships with others. And, second, to a considerable degree the strength and intensity of a relationship may not vary directly; for example, a child's relationship with her or his father may be the child's *strongest* family solidarity, but ordinarily, especially during infancy and early childhood, an individual's *most intense* relationship is with the mother; even the relationship with an older sister may be more intense than the relationship with the father.

The concepts of strength and intensity, taken individually and in conjunction, present certain problems of measurement. What follows are only suggestions about how to proceed in this regard. Strength is the easier of the two to measure. In speaking of measurements, one must (as with all social distinctions) be able to distinguish between ideal and actual patterns, that is, of strength in this case. The strengths of different relationships are to be measured in the context of other relationships, not on some absolute scale. Thus, given a relationship among individuals A, B, and C, if a conflict in instructions comes to C from A and B, C's relationship with A will be regarded as the stronger one if C follows A's orders and not B's. Ideally speaking, for members of the imperial Chinese family, there is no question but that the strongest relationship one had was with the head of the family. The Chinese were capable of quite elaborate calculations in these terms. Hardly a tale of family life exists in all of Chinese literature and history that does not involve conflicts between ideal and actual patterns of the strengths of solidarities.

The concept of intensity poses a double problem. In the first place, what is meant by the *degree* of an intensity? Intensity refers to emotions, affects, feelings—none of which is a clear-cut concept in social science. How does one measure "love" as an affect? Yet one unhesitatingly says (on either ideal or actual grounds) that individual C loves A more than he or she loves B. Again, the subjective point of view, defined ideally or actually, is invoked. In the second place, how does one compare intensities, for example, if one refers to two different intensities—respect and love—ideally and/or actually? Is love in some sense more intense than respect? Here again there is no hard-and-fast scale of measurement. Nevertheless, in one way or another all people make such distinctions, and, to quote W. I. Thomas, if men define situations as real (i.e., actual), they are real (i.e., actual) in their consequences (1928, p. 572). In trying to understand human behavior, what Sylvan Tomkins describes as the "positive affects" in some sense do take precedence over the negative ones (1962). Many classic plots of human conflict emerge from the fact that one can have a highly intense relationship with one individual and a stronger relationship, perhaps based primarily on respect, with another.

Finally, with regard to measurements of strength and intensity, there is the question of whether a relationship characterized by high intensity—especially of a positive kind—can override a relationship characterized more by strength. One may take refuge in the fact that such a contradiction is more likely to be the case actually than ideally. There would be no conflict if the relationship were not ideally stronger.

No readily applicable scale of measurement is offered here for either strength or intensity. And perhaps this lack should be discussed in chapter 3, because the lack of such a scale is certainly a sin of this book. I have nevertheless used these *concepts*° because, in one way or another, all people invoke them when they speak and think about social relationships. Or, perhaps to be more accurate, these are concepts one may use to make sense out of how people act, or even to predict how people will act under differing circumstances. One may predict, for example, that if a Chinese father tells his son to do one thing and his mother tells him to do another, he will do what his father dictates. Even in the absence of a clear-cut scale of measurement, the accuracy of such predictions is itself testimony to the fruitfulness of the distinction even when the scale of measurement remains implicit or, at the very least, highly inexplicit.

One further point about these two concepts: Neither the strength nor the intensity, as viewed by one party to the relationship, needs be identical either ideally or actually with the relationship viewed by the other. Thus, ideally speaking, a son's relationship with his father may be stronger than the relationships the son has with anyone else. It does not follow, however, that the father's relationship with the son is stronger than the relationships the father has with anyone else—his own father, for example. The relationship a daughter or son has with her or his mother may be quite different in the level and type of intensity by contrast with the intensity of the relationship from the mother's point of view. Again, these distinctions are possible both ideally and actually. No one thinks that mother love is identical to the love that offspring have for their mothers. Conflicts may arise over differing concepts of ideal and actual strengths and intensities, but there is no inherent conflict in the fact that these aspects of solidarity are not egalitarian. Indeed, friendship is the only widespread relationship in social history wherein these aspects are institutionalized as egalitarian (see pp. 58–59).

In this concern over the intensity of affects—how they might be measured and how distinguished and compared—*rationality*° has a special vulnerability quite apart from ignorance (*irrationality*°) and *arationality*°. Rationality is nonaffective. An invocation of rationality rests in the last analysis on a preference for, or love of, rationality—whether instrumentally or aesthetically based. Such biases are themselves affects rather than reasons. In this sense, an emphasis on any affect in and of itself can be carried to the extreme of an *ultimate end°*. One may be interested in knowledge for its own sake, art for its own sake, love for the sake of love, and so forth, but rationality generally requires justification on some other grounds than itself save for logicians and mathematicians. Rationality is generally instrumental—a means. Insofar as this is learned young, it, too, is taught by mothers.

However many variations have occurred in the ideal patterns of family life, the overwhelming commonality has focused on what may be described as eight possible relationships: husband-wife, father-son, father-daughter, mother-son, mother-daughter, brother-sister, sister-sister, and brother-brother. (Hsu 1971, esp. p. 8). No two of these relationships are likely to be so equally emphasized as a basis for solidarity among the members of a family as to be indistinguishable. Whenever family solidarities are oriented to the governance *and* continuation of a family, that is, to some form of stem or extended family system—which, in fact, has been the case for most human experience—one relationship will take precedence over all others: father-son solidarity. Even in recent times this continues to be true for most humans. An emphasis on the husband-wife solidarity suffices for the governance and continuity of the family while the children are relatively young. It does not, however, provide for succession. If that solidarity is emphasized, if the husband predeceases the wife, a female is left in charge of the family, not as a family regent but as a family head! In all known systems, while it has been possible for women to assume precedence by default, that has generally constituted a violation of the ideal patterns; but this pattern may not be immutable.

Mother-daughter, mother-son, sister-sister, and brother-brother relationships each violate one or both of the criteria of precedence and succession. The only relationship stably compatible with precedence and succession is the father-son relationship. It is the relationship internal to a family context that is overwhelmingly emphasized in all known societies that prize family continuity. For matrilineal societies, such a relationship may be replaced by uncle-nephew relationships that closely simulate father-son ones. One of the universals about premodern family structure is that more weight is placed on the strength of the father-son relationship than on any other family relationship. If succession is to be assured, the father-son relationship prevails over any other, including the one between husband and wife.

When family continuity beyond the rearing of an age cohort by a parental cohort ceases to be significant to those concerned, the precedence (in terms of strength) of the father-son relationship is weakened if not eliminated. In the family systems characteristic of modernized societies (i.e., multilineal conjugal family systems), the strongest family solidarity, ideally and actually, is that of husband-wife. But in such systems the family units are discontinuous (i.e., neolocal for both husband and wife), even if various other kinship units are not. In modernized societies, one's family of procreation is ideally different from one's family of orientation. But as human experience goes, this ideal exists for only a minority.

The picture is different insofar as the intensity of family solidarities is concerned. The intensity of mother-offspring solidarities is enormously greater than the intensities of other family solidarities. It is overwhelmingly probable that all initial human experience of solidarity is that which a neonate experiences with her or his mother. The content of that solidarity will vary according to the sex of the infant, as will its intensity, perhaps from the very earliest moment. However callous it may seem to speak of it, *nothing has been less likely in history than a precisely equal affective orientation to male and female offspring.* Both males and females generally display a preference for male offspring. It is therefore a reasonable hypothesis that this preference is reflected in the intensity of mother–child solidarity. In economic terms, if those are relevant, the mother's investment of affect in male offspring is likely to be greater than her affective investment in female offspring—and so, especially in terms of care of the aged, is the *income°* from that investment.

Whatever may be the case as far as the intensity of solidarity between a mother and male, as opposed to female, offspring, it is hardly open to doubt that the intensity of such solidarities is enormously greater than, and even predates, that of father–child solidarities. As between father and mother (if only because of the mother's relevance as a source of food for most neonates), neonates are overwhelmingly handled by mothers rather than by fathers. This continues even into modern contexts. *Mothers are more likely than fathers to initiate the development of solidarity with their offspring, and the experience of solidarity is likely to continue on a differentiated basis at least through the period of greatest helplessness on the part of the infants.*

The greater intensity of mother–child solidarity, together with the fact that such solidarity is maternally initiated, has a special implication for the *strength* of solidarities. As speculated above, father–son solidarity is ideally, and probably actually as well, the strongest one in the family system, certainly until modernized societies emerged. Similarly, father–daughter solidarity is likely to be the strongest solidarity for the daughter. But this must be qualified with regard to infant and childhood solidarities with parents. If a conflict exists between a mother's command and a father's, ideally, the paternal order will take precedence. But such deference has to be learned.

Solidarity patterns, like everything else, are initially learned by infants in a family context. Just as those family patterns underlie all subsequent nonfamily patterns— other things being equal, regardless of different treatment in other respects—all human beings, certainly until quite modern times, have experienced and learned about solidarities initially by their interactions with a mother.

The asymmetrically important maternal role regarding an infant's learning curve must be decisive vis-à-vis early learning of the strength of solidarities, as it is regarding practically all else. Thus, whatever the ideal patterns are concerning the strengths of solidarity over the general life cycle, until a child is taught to put someone other than the mother first, the strength of infant-mother solidarity must actually come first and be strongest if such strength is to exist at all. The mother therefore inculcates the desirability of alternative solidarities. Such inculcation requires specific learning about replacement itself *and, hence, further learning about hierarchy.*

Ironically enough, it is not odd that egalitarian treatment (even high evaluations of it) is so rare. *All human experience is initially hierarchical. The notion of egalitarian treatment, if it is to be learned at all, must be taught and learned as an exception, or alternative, to hierarchical treatment.*

At least until modern times, family universals, or any close approach to such, place overall emphasis on the strength of the other family members' solidarity with the father, who serves as family head (or with an uncle in some matrilineal societies). For this to obtain, the overriding strength of the mother-child solidarity, which is characteristic of initial socialization, must be specifically discontinued. *There is every reason to think that the mother herself teaches her offspring an alternative strength of solidarities.* Children everywhere have been taught by their mothers that the strength of their relationship with the father takes precedence over that with the mother. It is mothers who have taught offspring everywhere that father comes first. The future may see this changed, but it has nowhere yet been changed on any large scale.

Whatever the *strength* of family solidarities, the *intensity* of such solidarities is likely to be greatest in relationships with the mother; this includes the intensity of the relationship between the mother and her husband (or mate). There is a kind of *social inertia°* about this continued greater intensity of solidarities between mother and offspring. Although for many (perhaps all) societies, the initial strength of mother-child solidarity declines in relation to the solidarities that develop between father and child, there is no correspondingly general decline in the *intensities* of solidarity. It is not that these solidarities cannot be changed, but that they generally are not. There may be many reasons why this particular solidarity is not likely to be superseded by father-child or sibling relationships. The very importance, in family terms, of the political precedence of the father (or other male family head) may carry with it a concomitant sacrifice of warmth and intimacy. The development of comparable intensities between or among siblings involves not only problems of crossing the sex line but also those of crossing distinctions in absolute and relative age. In addition, given high infant mortality, an appropriate sibling relationship may simply not be available.

This is not to say that the intensity and strength of sibling relationships are irrelevant. Social scientists often distinguish between merit systems (sometimes called *universalistic°* criteria) and *ascribed°* characteristics (sometimes described as *particularistic°* criteria). Kinship criteria (*nepotism°*) overwhelmingly serve as the bases of all preferences and selections other than those made on the basis of merit. Of course, in the context of many, if not most, social systems, meritocratic selection has had little or no place, if only because the family context is so overwhelming a proportion of the entire social context for the vast majority of all individuals.

As an amusing derivative of this, for us, the term "nepotism" is vulgarly used to refer to favoritism in general. The two major types of kinship preferences in this respect are, of course, vertical relations among members of different generations, and horizontal relations among siblings, cousins, and so forth. Given the universality of particularistic criteria oriented to kinship, if any set of people had really achieved a one-child-per-marital-couple ideal, general social solidarities would have been difficult to maintain. Only "vertical," or intergenerational, solidarities would have been reliable. (This may become a major problem in the People's Republic of China [PRC] if its current demographic policies are successful.)

Within the family context, the universal picture changes radically when one considers the solidarity of offspring during childhood as opposed to infancy. Prior to modernization at least, a new form of sex-role differentiation was introduced at some relatively early point in childhood, say, by age four or five. At this point the male and female offspring were not only differently treated but also in some respects sexually segregated. Males tended overwhelmingly to come under the direct supervision and direction of older males, especially their fathers or brothers (if any). Females continued under the direct supervision and direction of their mothers and any older sisters.

This sexual segregation, of course, results in a marked and general difference in the rearing of males and females, but the difference is not simply a function of the segregation of sexes throughout the period of education for adulthood discussed above.[1] This practice also involves a radically differentiated experience in that *the intensity of solidarities between male children and adult or nearly adult males increases enormously, even though the intensity of their*

---

1. N.B.: Although initial education is not ordinarily sexually segregated, it is always sexually differentiated (see Axiom IV, pp. 19–20).

relationships with their mothers may remain greater than those with male family members or other males. Their interactions with the female members of the family are radically diminished. *By contrast, female development in family contexts is not radically discontinuous.*

Both male and female infants are literally weaned, but males are weaned from female direction and supervision and females are not. *Females tend to learn supervision and direction from both males and females. Males tend to learn male supervision and direction in place of female supervision and direction.* Of course, this is an easier speculation to maintain with regard to the ideal rather than the actual patterns. In the actual patterns of humankind, mothers and wives who dominate all of the members of their family, including the males—despite ideal patterns of patriarchy and the like—are and have been by no means uncommon. When this domination occurs, it does not vary at random to the fact that, initially, the strength and intensity of all infants' solidarities are much higher with female family members (especially the mother, of course) than with male family members.

Apart from the sex-role differentiation of infant and early-childhood solidarity, there is the question of sexual solidarity as such—considered puristically. The presumed universality of an incest taboo as an ideal pattern, even if often violated in actuality, radically diminishes the probabilities of family solidarities based on or directly related to sexual intercourse. Incest taboos in restricted cases are alleged not to have existed even as ideal patterns (although one may doubt the latter unless an *elite°* subset is involved). Even in such cases, relations between full brothers and sisters, fathers and daughters, and mothers and sons are probably regarded as taboo. If, in fact, this core of ideally tabooed sexual relations is not universal, then that generalization will be disproved. Inferences drawn from it, however, will still apply to the overwhelming majority for whom the taboo exists, at least as far as ideal patterns are concerned. Insofar as this taboo exists and is observed, sexual solidarity within the family context is possible between a husband (or equivalent) and one or more wives or as between a wife (or equivalent) and one or more husbands.

For the purpose of general analysis one may rule out generalized actual patterns of *polygamy*°, whether of the polygynous or polyandrous varieties. Even where *polygyny*° and *polyandry*° are clearly ideal patterns, the sex ratio of human beings at birth in all known societies prevents those patterns from being generalized. For all human beings on whom there are records, the sex ratio at birth is roughly one to one. For the average male (or female) to acquire two or more wives (or husbands) upon reaching adulthood, one must do something unusual, such as kill 50 percent of the males (or females), leave 50 percent of the males (or females) unmarried, kidnap women (or men) from other peoples, or have the males (or females) wait until age twenty-eight or thirty to marry and have the females (or males) marry at age fifteen and remarry immediately upon becoming widows (or widowers).[2] However spectacular the cases of sultans, for instance, with hundreds of women at their disposal, and despite much-varied ideal patterns in these respects, intercourse in a family context has been largely confined to one man and one woman, generally referred to as spouses.

As suggested above, husband-wife solidarity is certainly not the strongest one in the family context, unless

---

2. In cases of societies with many polygynous marriages, such unions are usually "postponed marriages" for young males and early marriages for young females and remarriages for widows. The postponed marriages for young males carry with them an important hierarchical distinction between married and unmarried males for the peoples concerned.

it is the only family relationship (e.g., in the case of a married couple who live apart from other kin and have no offspring). It is exceedingly unlikely, however, that the intensity is minimal; human beings certainly have varied all over the lot in their patterns in these respects. Ideal patterns of romantic love as the proper basis for marriage and the insistence on the right to individual selection—which are taken for granted by some peoples and become general in modernized societies—are not, as a rule, characteristic of all human societies.

But one does not have to be a Freudian or a sexual determinist to accept the proposition that acts of sexual intercourse are likely to be matters of high affectivity (or *cathectic°* intensity); that is to say, sexual relationships are not likely to be matters of indifference. Or, at least, if they are at first, they are unlikely to remain so. The affectivity of sexual relationships may underlie the extremely general apprehension that casual or contemned sexual relationships may threaten the stability of family patterns. Even the most latitudinarian peoples are alert to these potential interdependencies.

The intensity of sexual solidarities, even when they are not expected to be strong, may be evidenced by the overwhelmingly general experience that questions of family solidarity are enormously complicated when polyandry or polygyny is practiced. These complications are never confined solely to questions of who is, or (ideally) should be, having sexual intercourse with whom at any given time. Rather, they concern the strength and intensity of other family solidarities and of nonfamily solidarities, to the extent that the latter exist.

I have discussed universal, or well-nigh universal, patterns of solidarity as they involve infants and adults, children and adults, and adults and adults; however, I have not discussed infant-infant solidarities, or solidarities between or among young children or between the aged and infants, children, or adults. Infant-infant solidarity can for our present purposes be ignored, because in perhaps most family contexts in world history two or more infants have not been present to form such bonds; even had they been present, their limited mobility, command of language, and so forth, precludes the need to analyze any solidarity that does exist. Given recent findings about early human development, however, it is not out of the question that a great deal more examination of infant-infant solidarities in a family context may be required—more, at least, than now seems practicable or relevant.

Whatever may be learned of these solidarities, they are likely to be family ones, because infants—even in our most highly modernized contexts—spend so much of their time in family contexts. Family solidarities between young children and infant siblings have also not been taken up here, and neglect of these relationships, even given the present state of the art, would amount to the neglect of important questions. On the one hand, one might argue that in many family situations infants and children are not simultaneously present; hence, these solidarities are not relevant on the most general level. On the other hand, most people—prior to modernization at least—probably held strong preferences for high fertility. The major brakes on child-infant solidarities would have been high infant-mortality rates and the high mortality rates associated with childbirth, which, among other things, eliminated the immediate prospect of an additional infant or child. Nevertheless, such solidarities are not negligible, and the following generalizations can thus be presented.

Other things being equal, the most important of child-infant solidarities are likely to be those of female siblings with infants, regardless of the infants' sex. Older sisters are far more likely to be pressed into service as mother surrogates for their infant siblings than are their brothers.

Rightly or wrongly, morally or immorally, infant and child care falls almost exclusively into the category of "female work" for all relatively nonmodernized and most modernized societies alike, past and present. This distinction between "female work" and "male work" in general is an invidious one favoring males. Although infant and child care by female children constitutes a continuation of their participation in that part of the family context defined as "female," the male children in nonmodernized contexts switch their primary association early in childhood away from the female to the male members of the family and/or to other males.

Given the general preference for male offspring, female children taking care of infants are likely to learn this preference from their mothers. These children–infant solidarities will probably not be especially strong for two reasons. First, infants possess only a rudimentary consciousness, and thus experience, of solidarity. Second, female nurses or surrogates are overseen by their mothers and other older female family members. Thus, these relationships are far more likely to be intense than strong. Apart from the fact that female children cannot nurse their infant charges, there is every reason to think the infants respond as strongly to close affective attention from their sisters as from their mothers. Again, one would have to control for the affective involvement of the children with the infants. Although one might expect some difference between mothers on the one hand and sisters on the other, one may speculate that both mothers and older sisters supply considerable "affective attention."

Here again, as one would expect, male infants are destined to undergo a sea change during childhood—a change not experienced by female children, who are likely, rather, to experience relatively unchanged solidarities, save for the maturation of the infants and of their older sisters, and the departure to male contexts of their brothers. But in nonmodernized contexts infant brothers are destined sometime in childhood to leave the direct affective direction and attention of older sisters for that of their fathers and older brothers, if and insofar as any of those are present. Fathers are less often present in modernized contexts, owing to the separation of adult-male workplaces from the family contexts. Moreover, modern schooling practices mean that *older male siblings remain longer and more under the direct supervision of their mother and other females than they do in nonmodernized contexts.* Just as the affective intensity of solidarity with the mothers is likely to remain high after or during (perhaps especially during) this transition, one may speculate that the same would be true of the solidarities with older sisters.

If males and not females undergo a sea change, then all male children experience what are, from their point of view, important solidarities with both older brothers and sisters, if any. Using the same reasoning, females are much less likely to experience important solidarities with their older male siblings; this is probably more true of the intensity than the strength of solidarities. On the whole, females in childhood and beyond are not likely to have highly intense relationships with their older brothers.

Nevertheless, those relationships can be strong—especially in patriarchal and patrilineal contexts; family contexts are always institutionalized as patriarchal. The strength of the solidarity of sisters with their fathers takes precedence over solidarities with their brothers, although the latter are much stronger than their solidarities with sisters. In contrast, sister-sister solidarities are likely to be much more intense. The solidarities of brothers with older sisters are overwhelmingly likely to be more intense than strong.[3]

3. A sapient critic has pointed out that there is a sea change of enormous importance for most, if not all, females. That change is likely to take place as a result of marriage—granted that lies outside

Moreover, because of the greater role of female siblings in infant and child care, younger brothers are more likely to have relationships of high intensity with older sisters than vice versa. Here again there is a generally high level of asymmetry on the basis of sex.

I have said very little about the substantive content of family solidarities, save for references to mother–infant and mother–child inculcations and the role of fathers, in nonmodernized contexts, in directing and supervising their sons when their sex-segregated education for adulthood begins. From earliest infancy, however, if older sisters are present in the family context, learning and teaching are likely to be important parts of the substantive content of sister–infant and sister–child relations. When sisters take care of infant siblings, there is some learning at the very least from that very relationship. Such learning and teaching are much less likely to be true of older brothers at this stage of development. An important part of language learning, for example, is probably a function of sister–infant solidarities. For all of the use of language by older brothers relative to infants, the use of such language by older sisters must be enormously greater, given their greater involvement in infant and early-child care. Brothers may talk seldom with their infant siblings; sis-

---

the scope of this monograph, which concentrates on development up to or through the age of five. When marriage takes place, the female is more likely to leave her family of orientation and take up life in a new family context than is her husband. Her husband's family of procreation is far more likely to be a continuation in one form or another of his family of orientation. What is germane to this work is that, although such a change for females takes place at a different absolute-age distinction than the ones under consideration in general here, it is extremely likely that socialization with regard to this future set of events begins for females before they reach the age of five. *Quite apart from male precedence, or different from but closely related to it, is the sense of marginality thus inculcated on female children.*

ters probably talk a great deal with them. Sisters have such relationships with infant siblings of either sex. When older brothers have such relations, they are more likely to be with their male siblings.

In all of the literature and records on human beings, much is said of the aged. The general expectation was and remains that old people be cared for in some sort of family context. In fact, however, this expectation is more sentimental than generally fulfilled. Until the past century or so, the aged constituted only a small percentage of the total population. The problem of old age (and most of senescence, for that matter) was obviated by short life expectancy.[4] Until quite recently, life expectancies have not varied much from a norm of twenty-seven to thirty-one years of age. Sentimentality to one side, infant–grandparent solidarity is not likely to be one of considerable strength unless the grandparent is the family head or holds some similar position. Then, however (as noted above in the case of the father), the intensity of infants' solidarities is likely to be much more revealing than the strength of those solidarities.

The intensity of infant–grandparent solidarities is likely to have many more implications for the child's development than is any question of strength; this continues to be the case for extant solidarities between children and grandparents. The grandparent(s) concerned are likely to be in retirement of some sort. Given the ordinary precedences granted on the bases of age, generation, and sex, the strength of these solidarities from the grandparental point of view (that is to say, the extent to which the

4. For example, a population with a growth rate of 0.0 and a life expectancy at birth of 27.5 years for females and 24.9 for males would contain only 8.72 percent of people age sixty or more (Coale, Demeny, and Vaughn 1983, p. 286). Had the growth rate been −5, the percentage would be 10.52; had it been +5, the percentage would be 7.17.

grandparent would ideally or actually have to concede to and follow the wishes of the infant or child) is so trivially small as to be negligible or nonexistent.

Before modernization, with its concomitant increase in life expectancy, grandparents are always consigned to largely honorific and sentimental family roles.[5] The daily activities of the family members are never, save by default, a function of the presence of grandparents either in the family context or on its immediate periphery. With modernization the possibility of grandparental relationships changes radically, though, interestingly enough, the actuality does not. Where modernization is extensive, life expectancy at birth is radically increased, going quite readily to ages well in excess of sixty years, with the more highly modernized societies having life expectancies well above seventy years. Under these conditions most grandparents are likely to be alive not only through the infancy of their grandchildren but also through their childhood and a considerable portion of their young adulthood as well. Indeed, it becomes probable under high modernization that more individuals will live to see—if they wish to see—their great-grandchildren than have previously lived to see even their grandchildren.

In modernized contexts, however, grandparent-child solidarities are not as radically altered as one might expect, because relatively few grandparents actually live as members of their grandchildren's families of orientation. These solidarities are thus likely to be influential in only sporadic, ceremonial, ritualistic, and recreational ways. The intensity provided by these solidarities, in any event,

5. When grandparents, especially grandfathers, are present, their precedence, ideally speaking, is often quite strong. Such cases, however, are likely to be accompanied by retirement patterns. At the very least the aged are too honorific to be burdened with day-to-day decisions or to be held responsible for failures (Levy 1949, pp. 128–29; Levy 1952, pp. 318–19, 370–71, 482–86).

will be much more important. But the strength of such solidarities, both ideally and actually, continues to be limited.

Much greater differences for the family roles of grandparents exist in social contexts wherein modernization has not been achieved or is not far advanced, although sufficient access to modern medical technology will have doubled life expectancy at birth. In these relatively nonmodernized contexts, again, all the grandparents are likely to be available to form solidarities with their grandchildren. *Furthermore, ideal patterns that isolate grandparents from the families of orientation of their grandchildren have not yet emerged. A strong preference for patrilineality or matrilineality, however, may become vulnerable.* Under the impact of modernization, families become multilineal, and grandparents are almost certain to be present—either a matrilineal or patrilineal pair, or both—rendering grandparental solidarities with infants and children likely.

When such relationships emerge, they are accompanied by problems associated with increased longevity, which has almost always been regarded as a good thing, to wit: "The last of life for which the first was made." Again, the intensities of the relationships between grandparents and infants or children are likely to be greater than their strengths, although there is a complicating feature here. These grandparents have been accustomed not only to having strong relations with their children but also to precedence in such relations—a precedence they can no longer have now that their children are themselves parents. The possibility of conflict between grandparent-grandchild solidarities and parent-child solidarities is therefore likely to increase. One does and will observe all sorts of variations of these patterns because, with the increase of grandparents' survival rates there also goes a definite increase in the probability that grandparents will reside with their grandchildren, despite ideal patterns to the contrary.

Anyone who envisions a large or extended family, a vision that evokes a great deal of the world's family lore, will be impatient with the great emphasis placed thus far on parents, infants, and nonadult children. What of relationships in a family context between or among young adults, or adults other than the parents and infants or children? What of the relationships of young adults with one another in a family context?

As in the case of grandparents, these possibilities are actually considerably more restricted than the ideal patterns of extended or stem family systems would lead one to expect, if only for demographic reasons in those societies characterized by short life-expectancies. Granted, this is mostly a function of high infant mortality rates. Nevertheless, such high rates of mortality limit the possibilities of increased family membership via siblings whose families of procreation are continuations of their families of orientation.

Prior to modernization most ideal family patterns called for some form of stem or extended family system. I have presented hypotheses about that in the discussion of solidarity (see pp. 61–67). One cannot prove at present, however, that some form of extended family is either universal or even primordial. Evidence abounds that nuclear families have existed and do exist as ideal and actual patterns—quite apart from the unsound contention that the nuclear family *is* the universal ideal family pattern. Young-adult or middle-aged-adult solidarities that exist in actual family contexts are overwhelmingly confined to those between a young husband and wife or a more mature marital pair.

Incidentally, although divorce and remarriage are possible in many family contexts, it has been probable until at least the past century and a half that if a family relationship existed between middle-aged or elderly adults, it would be a continuation of a husband-wife relationship established earlier. When ideal family patterns call for the representatives of one sex or the other to have their families of procreation be continuous with their family of orientation, one might expect a substantial prevalence of continued relations between young, married adults and the parents of one or the other of the pair. Some people, of course, have had family patterns in which everyone's family of procreation is expected to be different from the family of orientation, in which case parents and their young married son(s) or daughter(s) would not ordinarily be living together.

When these relationships exist, they are likely to be strong, until or unless the older couple "retires." If family patterns are ideally patrilineal, the intensity and strength of the son's relations with his parents are likely to be a continuation of previous patterns. Relationships with her husband's parents are likely to be strong ones for the new wife (if the family is patrilineal and patrilocal) but considerably less *intimate*° than her husband's relations with his parents. Her relationship with her mother-in-law is likely to be more intimate than her relationship with her father-in-law.

Various other possible relationships loom even less large. Even if fertility is high among these peoples prior to the availability of modern medical technology, large numbers of children are unlikely to be present in the family context a great deal of the time. Infant mortality, miscarriages, and the like radically diminish these possibilities. Overall, few more than two siblings per marital pair survive to maturity. Because the sex ratio at birth of these individuals is approximately one to one, then, overall, roughly 25 percent of the families have two males surviving, another 25 percent two females, and 50 percent a male and a female. If these societies possess family patterns requiring neolocal residence for young married pairs and, consequently, separate families of procreation for each sibling, no uncles and aunts would be available to act in nuclear family contexts, though they might in more extended kinship arrangements. The greatest probability would be the presence of one uncle, if a patrilineal extended or stem family, or one aunt, if a matrilineal extended or stem family. Such family configurations are not likely to be long continued.

The incest taboo results in brothers or sisters either (1) marrying outside the family and starting new families or (2) entering older, but different, family contexts. The overwhelming majority of all people who live or have lived under these conditions are highly motivated to get married. When there is one daughter and one son, the daughter might, for example, marry out and join her husband's family of orientation or set up a new household; the brother would import a wife into the ongoing family context or himself set up a new family context. It is unlikely that two brothers would each bring a wife into the context and so complicate the picture. Under these demographic conditions, two brothers could do this if, and only if, the two-daughter families placed little emphasis on family continuity.

The net general result in the overwhelming majority of such cases is that the two-son families, in effect, trade one son for a wife for the remaining son, and that the two-daughter families, in effect, trade one daughter for a husband for the remaining daughter. In those families with one daughter and one son the daughter is, in effect, exchanged for a wife for the son. It is hard to escape the conclusion that the probability of *intrafamily*° solidarities involving uncles and aunts is restricted, despite ideal preferences for such relationships. Relationships among young adults in a family context are thus confined largely to (1) younger adult siblings prior to their marriages out of the family context, or to (2) a young husband (wife) and his (her) young wife (husband).

When two or more sons survive to maturity, keep in contact, and continue to be members of the same family, those relationships are likely to be strong—stronger than any other, in fact, except for the respective relationships each has with his father. Brother-brother relationships are likely to be more intimate than any of the father-son relationships; they are also likely to be more unstable. The relation between brothers is emphasized here because all these societies are patriarchal, so the power roles of males ideally take precedence over roles involving females. One may even suspect that although patrilineality is not universal, it is more widespread than matrilineality or multilineality. Insofar as that is the case, the relevance of fraternal as opposed to sororal relationships is vastly increased. In social settings apart from family contexts, males take precedence in general over females; therefore females more often achieve power and precedence as a function of who their fathers or their husbands are. In *interfamily*° relationships, or in nonfamilial contexts altogether (insofar as those exist), wherein more than 85 percent of the population spend upward of 85 percent of their waking and sleeping hours within eyeshot and/or earshot of other family members, comparative advantages are far more likely to be conferred by a network of solidarities among brothers or uncles or the like than on any other basis.

If one considers actual as well as ideal patterns, these comparative advantages are much increased if the general social context is characterized by an *open class*° system that places great emphasis on merit rather than by a *closed class*° system based, of course, overwhelmingly on particularism.[6] Even in the latter context, however, the com-

---

6. Because actual emphases on universalism (merit systems) tend always to break down in the direction of particularism, of which nepotism is the chief form, those with nepotistic opportunities in an ideally universalistic setting have a comparative advantage that those lacking nepotistic connections do not have. That is, they have a sort of "illegitimate" comparative advantage. In an ideally particularistic setting, whatever advantages are conferred by particularism, usually nepotism, are legitimate for all.

parative advantages of having many brothers who survive to adulthood is much greater than of having a corresponding number of sisters. There may be important exceptions to this as a function of whom those sisters marry, the importance of which will be buttressed by the fact that, even though brother-sister relationships are not likely to feature strong solidarities, they are likely to be quite intense and, if they exist are likely to have extended from the infancy of the brothers (see pp. 103–104).

These relationships are likely to be the more significant when the sister is older than the brother. Much is made of the responsibility and attachment of older brothers to younger sisters, but it is doubtful that those relationships have been nearly as significant as those between older sisters and younger brothers. One would expect this if only because *older sisters are far more likely, as I speculated earlier, to have a role in the socialization of younger brothers than older brothers are in the socialization of younger sisters.* There are probably few occasions in human experience in which older brothers play a significant role developing the initial part of the learning curve of younger sisters. *The role of females in child rearing is asymmetrical not only between mothers and fathers but also—less dramatically and less certainly but nonetheless pervasively—between sisters and brothers.* The fact that in all nonmodernized contexts young males at some point are transferred to the supervision of fathers or older brothers means that they are not as available to help with their junior siblings as are older sisters, who have remained under maternal supervision.

If one wishes to speculate on discontinuities with other mammalian species, one might fall back on the observation that although the solidarity patterns of lionesses acting in the context of a pride are vastly more significant in the socialization of young male lions than are adult male lions, young lionesses and young lions are equally involved in socialization of their younger brothers. Indeed, brothers and sisters, whether of the same or different litters, seem to have relationships that are not importantly differentiated by sex, at least until hunting patterns emerge. Closer attention to this matter may prove otherwise. It would certainly seem to hold that these differences exist among humans.

For examples of social relationships that appear, on surface observation at least, to be analogous to certain relationships characteristic of Homo sapiens, quite deliberate reference is made here to prides of lions, packs of wolves, and horse herds rather than to the extensive literature on nonhuman primates. These matters have not been precisely tied down by sociobiologists or biologists, or by sociologists and anthropologists. They are sufficiently removed from the behavior of Homo sapiens to make one pause and consider the extent to which these patterns, too, may well be matters of evolution. One cannot read about or view films of prides of lions, packs of wolves, or horse herds without thinking that these patterns of conduct are relevant to human conduct.

Furthermore, one may counter frequently met arguments with facts about some other mammalian behavior that would seem to contradict them. One of the oldest prejudices, perhaps on the wane now, in this connection is that the prominence of human males in hunting societies, given the comparative advantages of males in upper-body strength and quickness of reaction, led to their being selected out as hunters, and that fact was presumed to result in their establishing precedence in terms of power (i.e., political precedence) over females. Even assuming prehistoric humans were largely big-game hunters rather than "hunters and gatherers," it is by no means clear that a comparative advantage in killing big game is the basis for establishing precedence. That reasoning seems clearly contradicted by the apparent behavior of lions. Male lions certainly have greater upper-body strength than lionesses, and they may be quicker in their physical reactions. Lions do depend on the hunting of large game, but the male lions take a relatively small part in this hunting. Most of it is apparently done by the lionesses. This has not, however, enabled lionesses to establish political precedence, or anything remotely resembling it, over male lions. Quite the contrary, once the kill is made, the adult male lion asserts supremacy, even drives off the lionesses and cubs, eats his fill, and leaves the remainder for the rest of the pride. The actual roles of respective wolves in hunting, similarly, does not seem to determine the political patterns in the pack. The Alpha wolf is a male, except perhaps in cases of default when the Alpha male has been killed, no new Alpha male has emerged, and the Alpha female takes over.

One can, no doubt, find mammalian orders, maybe even humans, whose representatives are primarily gatherers, and yet the males give every sign of exercising power over females and the young. None of these matters has been elegantly tied down by sociobiologists. Rather a pity that! Why do lions pride and tigers not? Why do lions and lionesses behave so? To say that survival value explains it is to flirt dangerously with teleology in general and adaptionism in particular.

These examples have another relevance. Younger students in these fields will probably see radical advances in the next two to three decades. Those who investigate what does determine the behavior of lions, wolves, and horses are less likely to be deterred by arbitrarily assigned discontinuities between a social (or cultural) realm and a puristically biological one than are students of Homo sapiens or the "closer" primates. It was, after all, not so long ago that many hominids regarded themselves as radically differentiated from other hominids as a dependent function of skin color and other physical features. When one speaks of discovering an elegant biological reduction of why lions pride and tigers do not, one is not likely to be deterred by the question of whether the social (or the cultural characteristics) in question are permanently emergent properties of lions and tigers.

Some of the findings of modern ethologists seem to imply that sex-based role differentiation carried out from birth is not unique to the human species. Observers of horse herds report that colts and fillies are treated differently virtually from birth. The supposition is that colts are more aggressive both in seeking to nurse from their dams and in playing with the stallion who leads the herd. Both the mares and the stallions treat colts more aggressively than they treat the fillies. If these observations are correct, they argue that sex-based role differentiation is not unique to human beings, even in the context of infancy or early childhood. In the case of the horse herds, moreover, the explanation generally offered is an explicit biological reduction (i.e., hormonal differences in colts and fillies) and is in no way cultural.[7]

It should also be noted that, even in the case of horses, this cannot be considered an elegant scientific reduction but only a probable one. Despite all the pitfalls of arguing by analogy, this might suggest that even though the specific forms of role differentiation on the basis of sex may be "socially (or culturally) determined," the fact of differentiation may be explicable on puristically biological grounds. This is only to say that, at the present state of knowledge, it is easier to imagine a legitimate biological reduction of the "fact" of human sex-role differentiation than to imagine such a reduction of the particular forms that such a differentiation might take in any particular set of humans.

Aside from the aspects of solidarity that are in some sense internal to family contexts, the most general ques-

7. Daniel T. Rubenstein, Department of Biology, Princeton University, provided the information on horse herds.

tion of solidarity is posed by relationships with nonfamily members. The simplest observation regarding all peoples is that some such solidarities always exist. And their existence justifies confident speculation about the existence of a second membership unit (a subsystem of any human society), which would be some unit of *governance°*. This unit is not a subsystem of a particular family (i.e., not internal to any family).

Considerable social lore seems to suggest that the family is little if at all differentiated from the general communal context. This impression is particularly strong in the case of extremely *primitive societies°*, that is, societies with relatively few members, most of whom can therefore be directly acquainted and perhaps even related by kinship ties. The territory inhabited by the members of a primitive society at any given time is relatively small, and the members often live close to the subsistence level.

These peoples may interact with others who are considered members of different societies. Much modern research implies that interactions have been the case, but it can hardly be doubted that some peoples have lived and died without any such contact. Of course, direct evidence about the existence of such peoples would be rare indeed and hard to come by. It would likely be archeological. Nevertheless, one may speculate that *members of these, or any other, societies have always distinguished between family units and some more general social contexts.* Even if all members of a society are reckoned kin, they never all belong to one single family unit.

One critical question in this connection is whether the strength and intensity of some relationships with nonfamily members exceed those with family members. Alas, as with so many questions, the answer here is that they may or may not be. That is to say, members of some societies may prize solidarity with their chief, or king, or emperor, or shaman more highly than they do their solidarity with a family head or the like. There are also societies (like that of imperial China) for which, ideally speaking, the strongest social relationship one has is with the head of one's family. Even in this case, however, one might actually bow to the strength of the relationship with a nonfamily member, willy-nilly, especially if he were the emperor or his representative.

Imperial Chinese society may be a rarity in the extreme lengths to which its members went to institutionalize the precedence of family solidarities over any others. Nevertheless, all relatively nonmodernized peoples (even when certain nonfamily solidarities ideally take precedence over family ones) generally have the strongest solidarities with other family members. When this contradiction between ideal and actual patterns occurs—and it must have occurred often in human history—the individuals concerned not only must balance the strengths of conflicting solidarities but also must adjust to the discrepancies between their ideal and actual patterns of solidarity.

Despite the variation of ideal and actual patterns concerning the strength of solidarities between family members and nonfamily members, the picture is much more consistent with regard to intensity. It is overwhelmingly probable that for all relatively nonmodernized people (and even for all relatively modernized people) the intensities of their relationships with family members ideally and actually exceed that which they have with any nonfamily members—qualifying this for courtship, of course. Clichés observing that blood is thicker than water are not rare. Of course, such assertions do not demonstrate this point definitively and may apply as much to the strength of solidarities as they do to the intensities. So, if one prefers flatly deterministic rather than probabilistic statements, one may phrase the matters thus: *Ideally and/or actually, family solidarities are characterized by greater intensities than are nonfamily solidarities.* That is certainly true of mother-infant and mother-young child relationships.

The precedence of family over nonfamily intensities would follow from the same factors asserted above, where it was noted that some intrafamily intensities are higher than one would expect given the distribution of strengths of solidarities internal to family structure (see pp. 68–80); it would also follow from the intensity of solidarities during infancy and young childhood on the one hand and of more or less regularized sexual intercourse on the other. Neither of these intensities is ordinarily encountered in nonfamily relationships. Whatever the communal participation in infant care and child rearing, most, especially for infants, is handled in family contexts by mothers; most of all other activities for nonmodernized people are, of course, also handled in family contexts. Even for the most modernized people, the care of infants and young children is also carried out in family contexts by mothers.

Similarly, premarital and extramarital sexual practices may generate affects as intense as those that characterize family contexts. This is precisely one of the two reasons why, in all known societies, sexual intercourse, even in its most meretricious, instrumental, casual, and least directly affective forms, is never viewed as totally irrelevant to family considerations.[8]

Affective neutrality in relation to infant care, child rearing, and/or sexual intercourse is never achieved, even if attempted. A total affective neutrality in such contexts, if it could be achieved, would be regarded as pathological in the context of any society. It is likely that the impact of affective neutrality on infants and children would be radically selected against in the clearest Darwinian sense. Vio-

---

8. The other is that sexual intercourse may result in issue, thus shifting a "sexual intercourse" kinship unit to one oriented at least in part to biological descent *and* sexual intercourse—that is, a family unit, however illegitimate, unexpected, or unorthodox.

lence in family contexts is very much a matter of affect, whether approved or not. Genuine apathy in family relationships is much rarer and is almost certainly much more disturbing to those who witness it than is violence. It is not a matter of accident that down through history and across every social (or cultural) variation high intensity of affect among individuals in a family context is taken for granted in a manner not characteristic universally of any other organizational context for all societies.

The initial socialization of solidarity is mother-taught on mother-time, and this continues to be true for the vast majority of the patterns of solidarity inculcated on the individual throughout early childhood.

7

Political Allocation

The allocation of power and responsibility in family contexts is separable only analytically from the subject of solidarity. This chapter is thus a repetition, with different emphases, of the discussion in chapter 6 concerning the strength of solidarities in a family context. Political allocation in family contexts is always hierarchical. This is the most general statement that can be made. Family relationships are not friendships as such—to wit, the saying: "You can pick your friends, but you can't pick your relatives." Even when spouses choose one another, the resulting relationship is not egalitarian, and even when egalitarianism can be perceived as an ideal pattern, the actual patterns reflect hierarchical distinctions.

The universal bases for precedence in family contexts are age (broken down into distinctions of absolute and relative age), generation, and sex (see pp. 53–58). Age and generation are basic distinctions in all societies—at least, the ones under consideration here are basic—and sex is always a specialized one. Nothing is less likely than that claims to precedence be precisely balanced on the bases of age, generation, and sex.

In the event of apparent contradictions in precedence, generational solidarities are far more likely to prevail over those based on age or sex. For example, in no known society (unless it may be said to hold for extremely recent cases) can it be said that, ideally speaking, women are supposed to occupy the highest positions of power. Actually speaking, when the traditionally male positions of authority are left vacant, as in the early death of a family head while the offspring are still infants or children, the mother, or perhaps an aunt, is exceedingly likely to take succession. In imperial China, for example, it was ideally held that, prior to marriage, a daughter was subject to her father, as a wife to her husband and a widow to her son. Strong-minded widows who dominated their sons and ruled effectively in their family contexts were, however, not rarities in Chinese history.

In general, if the situation is stable, the different bases of political precedence reinforce rather than contradict one another. In order to avoid discussing all of the possible permutations and combinations capable of producing political precedence, I would like to offer the following observations: Other things being equal, family heads are always distinguished by, and are likely to represent, the oldest absolute-age set in the family context (except for those who have retired). Family heads are also likely to be relatively older than any other family member, save for retired persons, and usually belong to the oldest generation in that family context (again with the exception of retired persons). Finally, the family head is male. Even in contexts where males are educated in sexual practices by older women, they overwhelmingly tend to cohabit with women of their own age or younger.

Those who are habituated to highly modernized contexts view such allocations of power and responsibility as largely concerned with "family matters." One must not forget, however, that for the vast majority of all peoples past and present, "family matters" encompass most matters. Never did more than a small minority operate totally (or nearly so) outside family contexts; this holds even for societies characterized by the presence of many priests, nuns, soldiers, and so forth.

Even when individuals operate in a nonfamily context, it is overwhelmingly probable that they operate under some direction and supervision by family members. Thus, if one acts in a nonfamily context, one is likely to do so as a family member and, further, to be supervised by family members while doing it. With the exception of relatively modern contexts, one is still not likely to be out of eyeshot and/or earshot of other family members even when operating with nonfamily members. The relevance of one's family to one's behavior in nonfamily relationships is not likely to be small. Even when one operates in settings isolated from family contexts, the relevance of one's behavior to family contexts is likely to be extremely important in understanding one's behavior. Problems of various sorts always arise if that relevance is opaque (see pp. 43–45).

One may generalize about political allocation as follows: *When the locus of power is not balanced by the locus of responsibility, the result is inherently unstable.* If one has power for which one cannot be held responsible, one is extremely likely to exercise ("abuse"?) that power capriciously. That is, this kind of power is likely to be wielded in such a way that the results are ineffective for the purposes sought and are also destabilizing, *if only because of ignorance.* This destabilization does not need to be freighted with connotations of "good" or "bad." Correspondingly, if one is responsible for performing functions but lacks the requisite power, one is likely to perform in an ineffective and destabilizing manner—at least to the degree that the performance relates to stability. Again, no judgment about the value or worth of stability is made here.

Instability, as a function of the exercise of power for which one is in no way accountable, is more likely to follow from capricious applications of power than from other sources. One may, for example, require performances of one's subordinates that they cannot deliver or that, if delivered, are destabilizing. If one cannot be held responsible, one cannot be stopped. Even in the absence of figures who can be stigmatized as evil—madmen, for instance, who sadistically fiddle while Rome burns— sooner or later, those exercising power will do so capriciously, if only out of ignorance.

It matters little from this general point of view whether the lack of knowledge is avoidable. Sooner or later, any wielder of power will make an incorrect assumption about where a particular exercise of power will lead. Some of those mistakes will lead to instability. The more interdependent the system, the greater the risk—this is true regardless of how one values instability. If there is a mechanism that renders the wielder of power accountable, then there is always at least the possibility that that mechanism can be invoked in time to halt a capricious use of power and, therefore, "set things right." *Once launched on a disaster course, then the correction of that course is itself capricious—if, in fact, one is in no way accountable.* This is one of the two great problems in maintaining stability when charismatic leaders are in control.[1] If launched on a disaster course, the charismatic leader can be stopped only if he or she is killed or if, for whatever reason, that *charisma*° is lost.

A critical problem for political allocation in kinship terms is, therefore, the question of how, in the last analysis, the power of the family head is balanced by responsibility. It is the classic question of who guards the guards themselves. Two general forms of such balance can be found in social history—one empirical, the other nonempirical. The first involves the accountability of family heads to individuals outside the family. Of course, this leads directly into some nonfamily pattern of governance, a major form of which has, in turn, involved accountabil-

---

1. The other is the difficulty of providing for succession.

ity to kinship councils, clans, and so forth. Although these are kinship units, they are nonfamily ones. Another of empirical balance is accountability to individuals who are neither kin nor family. When these relationships exist, some general form of governance (patterned either after family or kinship contexts) must also exist so as to legitimate authority on some basis besides kinship. In either case, the unit concerned must be regarded as the legitimate locus for the settlement of interfamily disputes and/or other disputes among other social units. However legitimate such "governments" may be, they are not necessarily "strong" enough to settle such disputes. They are especially prone to instability when they are not.

In each of the above cases, however, the balance of power and responsibility is explicitly empirical. A given individual is or can be called to account by others, acting either as individuals or as representatives of other organizations. These matters are institutionalized in varying ways, but common to all of them is that, *if the systems are stable, the aspects of* conformity° *are likely to be high even if the* sanction° *aspects are weak.*

A second form of balanced power-responsibility, however, appears to be both common and highly effective. It is obtained by nonempirical orientations of the family head and other family members. A scientific observer can say nothing at all about whether nonempiricals exist or are effective in balancing power and responsibility or in "doing" anything else. One can nevertheless observe empirically that a given actor *believes in* (or at least acts as though he or she believes in) not only the presence but also the effectiveness of nonempiricals.[2] One cannot scientifically observe that one's ancestors influence this world, but one *can* observe whether most imperial Chi-

---

2. One may quote W. I. Thomas: "If men define situations as real, they are real in their consequences" (1928, p. 572).

nese believed their ancestors to be endowed with powers and that their greatest obligation to the ancestors is to produce, and provide for, posterity. The head of an imperial Chinese family may appear to have had unlimited powers, but how he behaved vis-à-vis other family members was clearly limited by and patterned after the extent to which he believed his primary obligation was to secure the succession of the family so that the ancestors might be honored. Such nonempirical balances of power and responsibility point directly to the interdependency of religious aspects with other aspects of social life. Of course, such balances of power are likely to be particularly relevant to family considerations, if only because family considerations constitute the overwhelming proportion of all considerations for all people until the most modern times.

Because most family life (until modernization intervenes) is lived out in highly self-sufficient, local contexts, and because capriciousness as a function of ignorance is no less likely to be the fate of such people than of others, it can be assumed that most balances of power and responsibility in family contexts are probably internal to that context. Insofar as such families are stable and capricious exercises of power are avoided, they may easily be explained by explicit empirical considerations or by the implications of generally inculcated nonempirical orientations. In either case, when people act in terms of such patterns, the latter are in turn likely to have been inculcated on the individual in family contexts. For the most part (until modernization intervenes), whatever it is that enables families to be stable is itself "family-produced." *Until modernization intervenes, whatever enables stability in general to persist is also generally "family-produced." All infants and young children originally learn about such things from their mothers.*

This family-produced stability holds true regardless of one's evaluation of stability. The great majority of all people of all times, however, prize stability quite highly—and this includes even those who regard themselves as especially preoccupied with creativity and change. It takes a figure like Mao Tse-tung, who apparently believed in a state of continual revolution, to make one understand how reluctant, in general, people are to live in continual chaos—continuous, unremitting, and unpredictable change—that is, to change for change's sake.

For human societies there is a special irony down through history: *If one controls for other factors on which precedence is based, women never, ideally speaking, take overall political precedence over males.* Even in matrilineal contexts, uncles or brothers of roughly the same age take precedence over their sisters. Because more societies in world history are likely to be patrilineal than matrilineal, the families of procreation of some individuals are much more likely to be continuations of the families of orientation for males than for females. It holds true of females in the exceptional case, whereas in the "normal" case it holds for males. Wives are, in general, supposed to be subordinate to their husbands or, if not to their husbands, to their older brothers or some other patriarchal arrangement.

Although, universally speaking, overall precedence in family contexts is taken by males over females, it is equally true—in fact, true beyond peradventure of a doubt—that both males and females receive their basic (certainly their initial) indoctrination about political precedence from females—specifically, their mothers. If young boys are destined to be rulers, whether benign or tyrannical, they are overwhelmingly prepared for such leadership, and taught how to act accordingly, initially by women—above all, by their mothers and older sisters, if they have the latter. *"Male chauvinism" (or at least male precedence) seems to be inculcated on males and females down through all of history and in all social (or cultural) variation— through any and all* thick descriptions[o3] *of peoples—by females from birth.* This has, of course, no necessary implications for what should or should not be.

There is no known tenable (let alone elegant) biological reduction of either the universal trait of hierarchy or male precedence. It cannot be inferred from that lack, however, that the presence of hierarchy and male precedence, or the inculcation of both by females, is simply an arbitrary cultural (or social) artifact—that is, simply a function of inadequate social inventiveness. A great deal of new knowledge would have to become available to establish either proposition.

As regards relations with nonfamily members, at least two considerations guarantee for all peoples at all times that such relationships will always exist: First, the need to establish some form of interrelationship or interdependency among the members of two or more families is the general basis of nonfamily governance for all peoples— even when conducted by a royal family for whom kinship considerations are extremely important. From the point of view of any of the nonruling members, governance is on a nonfamily basis. Second, some sort of incest taboo is a strongly held ideal pattern for all known peoples. The core of the taboo, ideally speaking, prohibits father-daughter, sister-brother, and mother-son matings for the society's general membership. Even when the taboo is violated, legitimate marriages based on such relationships are exceedingly rare. When incestuous matings

3. "Thick description" is a term coined by Gilbert Ryle and given general currency by Clifford Geertz (Geertz 1973, pp. 6–10). A similar idea is attributed by Clyde Kluckhohn to Bronislaw Malinowski. Kluckhohn describes it as "the well-documented anecdote set firmly in a ramified context" (1943, p. 214). As developed by Malinowski and cited by Kluckhohn, the concept does not have the anti–intellectual and antiscientific connotations it has acquired in current usage.

are legitimated, the families involved usually will constitute an elite subset of the general set of families of the society—most often royal families and the like.

Societies may vary as to whether an individual's family of procreation is continuous with his or her family of orientation or whether it is a newly formed family unit (i.e., neolocal) for both males and females. In the former case, either the male or the female marries out of the family of orientation and into that of his or her spouse. In the latter, both males and females marry out of their families of orientation. In all these cases, however, for legitimate marital arrangements to take place, contact and interdependencies must somehow be established among family members and "outsiders."

The individuals who marry may be ideally related by kinship,[4] as in the case of "cross-cousin" marriage systems and the like. Ideally speaking, though, they are never members of the same family. And even when they are ideally related by kinship, demographic factors alone will prevail against the likelihood of such relationships becoming the actual norm for most couples (Kunstadter et al. 1963).

The general certainty that, one, some members of different families will interact and that the harmony of such interactions is not given *a priori*; two, marital formations are universal; and three, at the time of marital formation the spouses are never living totally outside family contexts—all lead one to conclude that family members are everywhere and always involved in *family foreign relations*°.

This involvement of family members is notably not the case for some mammalian species characterized by patterns that, at least intuitively, resemble those of families.

4. For the distinction between family units and other kinship units, see above, p. 42.

That is, sooner or later lions come to lionesses from different prides, and a takeover of the pride by a strange lion may, in addition, result in the ejection of adult, and even junior, lions from the pride. This does not mean, however, that the members of the pride (if they can be described as "family members" for these purposes) are thereby involved with the members of the "strange" lion's pride of orientation.[5] In other words, human spouses do not come to one another totally outside a family context. There are exceptions, but these are relatively rare. Improved knowledge of the ethology of mammals may eventually disabuse us of the idea that this trait is peculiar to humans.

There remains the problem of generalizations about solidarities that involve neither family members nor the formation of new family bonds, as with mating practices. Many such relationships, though not family relationships, involve kin. Problems of transportation for most peoples make for a concentration of both *affinal*° and *consanguine*° kin. Many individuals who are not members of one's own family are related by varying forms of kinship bonds. It is extremely difficult to generalize about these bonds because, here, the possible permutations and com-

---

5. There may be some semblance of interpride relationships for lions. Modern ethologists estimate that in as many as 52 percent of cases a pride will be taken over not by one lion but by fraternal littermates. In such cases, of course, two members of the strange lion's pride of orientation are involved, but from their entry into the new pride until their later death(s) or expulsion no relationship with any other members of their pride of orientation is involved. Thus, it would seem to continue to hold that although prides of lions are, in many respects at least, closely analogous to human families, the governance of lions involves no necessary social structure for lions outside the context of the pride. For human beings, as observed above, this is not the case. It may be, however, that in the case of other animals than Homo sapiens, the acquisition of mates does involve an equivalent of interfamily dependencies. Ethology is after all an infant science.

binations—even under the kind of demographic dispensations that have existed through world history for most people for most of the time—are extremely various.[6]

The most general way to differentiate these kinship bonds is to distinguish between those that, ideally speaking, take precedence over family relationships from those that do not. Other things being equal, even when kin relationships (e.g., between the head of a lineage and another lineage member) take precedence over a member's relationship with other family members, the *intensity* of one's nonfamily kinship relations is not likely to be as great as the individual's relations with family members. The possibility of conflicts between other kin considerations and specific family considerations is lessened by the fact that, for the vast majority of people for the vast majority of human history, behavior in broad kinship contexts is far less frequent than behavior in family contexts. Nevertheless, the possibility of conflict exists whenever nonfamily kinship relationships threaten to involve stronger solidarities than family relationships. Even when this is not ideally the case, the possibility of conflict remains. Most of any individual's kinship behavior is family behavior. That holds true for all societies, including modern ones.

The nonfamily kinship relationships most relevant to an understanding of general human history have been those of descent units, rather than those of sexual intercourse (see p. 42). These nonfamily kinship relationships always have to do with the place of family structure in the more general social structure. For nearly everyone throughout history, family membership has been the

6. One must, after all, keep in mind that although, by definition, kinship relationships are always oriented at least in part to biological descent and/or sexual intercourse, they are never solely determined by those factors.

most important element in determining social placement; nonfamily kinship membership, especially membership in descent units, is the next most important.

This is true for all classes, bridging distinctions between closed class and open class systems, and is another generalization that has not varied as a function of *class structure*° or class interests. But, because the placement of family members in closed class systems is a function of kinship in general and family membership in particular (whereas that may be true only of initial placement in open class systems), the kinship factor will loom larger there. Even in open class systems with a high actual approximation of ideal patterns, the actual relevance of kinship considerations to social placement can never be confined to initial social placement alone. As already discussed (see pp. 41–44), ideal and/or actual family contexts influence one's behavior in every other social context—this considered even apart from the fact that at least the initial part of every individual's learning curve is inculcated in family contexts.

It is much more difficult to generalize about kinship structure than about the family in particular; even more difficult in this respect are *non*kinship relations. At the present state of the art, it is extremely difficult to generalize about nonkinship solidarity—even for the "smallest" societies (so defined by the number of members and the territory they inhabit). Two generalizations are obvious enough, however: (1) These nonkinship solidarities must always concern the place of family patterns among more general social patterns, and (2) what happens to an individual in family contexts invariably conditions, if not determines, how he or she behaves in nonkinship contexts—that is, whether it is "supposed" to or not (see pp. 43–45).

The reverse is not true unless, at some level, everything that happens to an individual is relevant to every other behavior. That is: *All peoples must have some nonkin-*

ship relationships; indeed, there must even be some nonkinship relationships not oriented to the formation of kinship relationships. Nonkinship relationships oriented to the formation of kinship ties are obvious enough. As a minimum, these would relate to the selection of mates, adoption patterns, and so forth. The other nonkinship ties have, as a minimum, to do with the general patterns of governance. The most general distinction here is between societies whose ideal patterns hold family solidarities to be stronger than any nonfamily solidarities and societies not so characterized; the former seems to have been the case for imperial China. More general, however, are societies in which some nonkinship solidarities take precedence over any kinship solidarities, including family ones. These societies may range from extremely weak and ineffective forms of centralization to the most encompassing forms of *absolutism°*.

Until recently in human history the highly (or "completely") centralized forms of absolutism have been discussed more often than practiced. Prior to modernization, the great majority of all people lived in highly decentralized contexts; representatives of the society's government rarely intruded on the day-to-day activities of family members. Even if a king or emperor could take absolute precedence by exercising his prerogatives, he rarely did.

This exercise of kingly prerogatives varies, however, with the structure and frequency of elites, but then the elites of any society constitute a distinct minority. None of the highly centralized, nonmodernized empires—all founded by charismatic leaders—long survived the death of their founders. The more localized the behavior, the more likely it will be that family solidarities will explain most, if not all, of the action. Other things being equal, however, nonkinship solidarities are the most likely ones to conflict with family solidarities. For most of human history, such conflicts do not arise in substantial form for most of any population, and family solidarities determine most behavior. With the onset of modernization, al- though family solidarities remain most generally relevant, they become irrelevant to most of one's behavior outside family contexts—ideally speaking, at least. Of course, this is not the *actual* case, even for moderns.

NONFAMILY GOVERNANCE:

MINIMAL UNIVERSAL

"FAMILY FOREIGN RELATIONS"

All human beings live in terms of subsystems of either a single society or the interdependence of two or more so- cieties. Ordinarily, it is the former. All societies will be peopled, however, by members of two or more families. An incest taboo carries with it an inevitable consequence of family interdependence. Even if there were no such ta- boo, however, one could avoid this interdependency only by positing completely isolated, self-sufficient, single- family units. There are no records of such peoples.

In the foregoing discussion, I have explored some of the implications of the existence of such units for the strengths and intensities of the solidarities of family members. But what of the picture considered the other way around? One assumes or asserts the existence of some unit that, though it may be in and of itself a family unit (e.g., the family of a king), is nevertheless differenti- ated from its interdependent family units in that it is re- garded, ideally and/or actually, as the proper locus for the resolution of differences, or for leadership, or for what- not. Such a unit, then, for the members of these interde- pendent family units, is a *government*° in the sense in- tended here.[7]

7. Neither families nor governments seen as systems of action rather than as sets of individuals "do" anything. Individuals or sets of individuals do things to one another in terms of families or govern-

The family possesses, as argued above, a definite primacy, especially regarding the care and rearing of human beings. But government representatives also exhibit varying strengths and intensities in their solidarities with members of the society. There are two major possibilities: Either the strength of solidarity with the leader of the government prevails over any other strength of any other relationship, or it does not. (The connotations of "government," as generally used today, may be too strong to be applied to the most generalized forms of governance common to all human beings; "monopoly of the legitimate use of force" certainly does not exist in most of these contexts—either ideally or actually.)

In view of evolutionary possibilities, it would be parsimonious to speculate that at least the earliest forms of solidarities were based on family ties that took precedence over those between family members and members of any governing body. Generally, strengths cannot be marshaled for these governing bodies in the way that they can be marshaled for a given family context or a coalition of them. Still, one cannot rule out the possibility that the members of some systems, at least ideally speaking, have prized the solidarity of individuals with the ruler more than they have prized such ties with family members.

Regardless of how these strengths are aligned, it is overwhelmingly probable that a government leader exercises authority over a given member of society through that individual's family context—through a family member. That is to say, prior to modernization, individuals were more likely to be governed, indirectly, through family heads, or councils composed of family heads, or the like, rather than through a direct relationship with

---

mental patterns or any of varying combinations of the two. To speak of families or governments as "doing things" or "acting" is to commit the pathetic fallacy in its most general and frequent form in social analysis.

government representatives—which one takes for granted today. Even today, of course, family members mediate relations between government representatives and "minors."

With so much of life carried out in family terms, it is hard to see how things could be otherwise. An alternative to such family mediation may hold for individual, idiosyncratic relations, but continued, prolonged, or oft-repeated situations cannot have been handled that way because none could have been handled without directly affecting other family members. Simple governments are likely to function at the local or *neighborhood°* level, and their representatives are likely to govern through families. *The precedence of government representatives, like precedence within the family context itself, will function according to age, generation, and sex.* Of these three, however, *generation is often irrelevant,* because the government representative and the family member may have no common ancestors from whom generational descent can be traced.

Sex-role differentiation, as discussed earlier, is critical and universal. Never mind whether it should be so or not! In the past males took precedence over females, save by default, and continue largely to do so even in the present. Again, never mind whether it should be so or not![8] These differentiations leave variations in the relationship between ruler and the (in some sense) ruled that are largely based on age, apart from whatever qualities that establish the ruler's precedence as such. Thus, it may very well be that only the descendant of a particular individual can legitimately rule, but his precedence would vary most importantly with age. To the extent that this is true, provisions for some form of regency would need to be established in the case of infant or child rulers, some

8. For the moment, no one knows whether this can or will be changed for the future. If it is, the change will be as revolutionary as any in history.

sort of retirement for aged rulers, and some simulation whereby appropriate age differences are established between ruler and ruled if these are, in fact, chronologically absent. It is a testimony to the influence of Freud that we no longer need him to point us to the frequency of the metaphor of the ruler as a mature "father figure."

The present state of knowledge does not permit reduction of male and female behavior to puristically biological factors. Thus, the foundations for much, if not most, characteristic performances must be initially learned in a family context during infancy and childhood. Similarly, in the absence of any elegant sociobiological reduction (however often promised or threatened), the bases for behavior in governmental contexts must also be overwhelmingly family-taught and -learned, at the very least initially. The fundamental instruction is performed by mothers.

As asserted earlier, father-son solidarity is overwhelmingly likely to be viewed as the most critical one in the family context—ideally speaking.[9] In spite of this, fathers emerge as the "first outsiders" as far as infants are concerned. This father-son solidarity provides an analogy that underlies the basic patterns of governance; it is not a matter of chance that the ruler is so often regarded as the "father" of his people through so many social (or cultural) variations. The high, even extreme, emphasis so often placed on the virility of such rulers would seem to go right along with such an interpretation. Most people throughout world history have lived on the margin of demographic subsistence and have nevertheless desired numerous descendants (no doubt partly because they were

9. N.B.: This is not inconsistent with the actual critical nature of the mother-infant or mother–young child (male or female) relationship insisted on above. What people everywhere have held to be most critical need not in fact be most critical, though that belief may in and of itself have far-reaching implications for action.

unable to have them); thus, the precedence of a ruler would be reinforced by attributions of potency, preferably evidenced by the survival of an unusually large number of offspring.

Unless one assumes a discontinuous evolution for the human species and/or that the social (or cultural) is a permanently emergent property of humankind (that Homo sapiens has somehow been placed "but little lower than God" [Ps. 8:5]), *systems of government developed out of family contexts and on family models, never vice versa.*

Although hierarchical behavior has not been elegantly reduced to puristically biological explanations, it is assuredly universal for Homo sapiens. In addition, other mammals do not rear their young on egalitarian terms. Attributions of egalitarian patterns to nonhuman species as anything like a general pattern are among the least supportable of all pathetic fallacies. The general attribution of egalitarianism to the human species is not a pathetic fallacy, although it is an empirical one. Insofar as one cannot account for the inculcation of hierarchical patterns in puristically biological terms, one must fall back on the statement that such inculcations are not only social but are also carried out by mothers in a family context. With the development of what is here called governmental contexts, the hierarchical pattern is transferred to that context preponderantly on the basis of a family or kinship analog.

This emphasis on the governmental context for political allocation generally, and hierarchy specifically, has a special feature. In the development of human organizations, governments represent the original and universal— but nevertheless specialized—organizational contexts. Possible organizational foci include economic allocation, political allocation, solidarity, and so forth, but family organizations are clearly nonspecialized. The family is the quintessentially *basic* human organization. Even in the most modern contexts it is not a predominantly economically (as opposed to politically) oriented unit. As pointed out above, the family is not even predominantly oriented to solidarity (see p. 61).

The family as a general form of organization is quintessentially nonspecialized. It is not specialized with regard to child rearing, food preparation, exercise of leadership, teaching, or any of these matters—all are carried out in the family context. Governmental organizations are, however, always in some degree specialized with regard to allocations of power and responsibility. Governmental organizations are, hence, always specialized to some degree with regard to hierarchy. *Governments, however tenuous, constitute the quintessentially basic, specialized membership units for all societies.* In this sense, units that have a predominant political specialization are far more general than, say, units with a largely economic specialization, notwithstanding all we have to learn from Marx.

Families may be viewed as all things to all people in some contexts; governments never are. Just as fathers are the first "outsiders," government, however loosely organized, is the first "outside organization," and absolute rulers have never seemed to understand this. As Machiavelli and others so well understood, government leaders will be unavailing if they do not know how the behavior of others is relevant to the stability of their governments. Leaders must also be cognizant of their own allocations of power and responsibility, and how these are relevant to the possible existence of others and especially to the existence of family systems.

Again, the initial patterns forming the bases for all these matters are inculcated on infants and young children in a family context by their mothers.

8

Economic Allocation

The close connection between the strengths and intensities of solidarity aspects and political aspects in family contexts is obvious enough. But economic allocation is concerned most directly with strategic aspects of the substantive content of solidarities. It is necessary, however, to avoid implicit statements that would make these aspects of behavior appear to be "different things"—to be concretely different one from the other. *These aspects refer not to different things but to different ways of looking at the same thing.*

In speaking of economic aspects, one may conventionally distinguish between production and consumption—a distinction that is more curious than is generally appreciated. It is an analytic distinction within an *analytic structure°. What is viewed as production from one point of view is regarded as consumption from another.* The concepts are curiously analogous to the distinctions between *anabolism°* and *catabolism°* and between power and responsibility. Anabolism from the point of view of a parasitic vine on a tree is catabolism from that of the tree. Power from one point of view is responsibility from another. Production from the point of view of an automobile firm is consumption from the point of view of a steel (or plastics) firm.

Given the great talent for specialization in modern times, people have tended to *reify°* the concepts of production and consumption just as they have reified the concepts of economic and political allocation. Production is generally viewed as in some physical sense distinct from consumption. Similarly, in a vulgar sense, families are called "consumption units" and manufacturing firms are called "production units." For most human beings throughout most of human history, most production has taken place in family contexts, as has consumption. To confuse production and consumption with concretely different activities is not only vulgar but also misleading.

It is misleading to think of the family, even in the most highly modernized contexts, simply as a unit of consumption, as though it existed without reference to production, save for nonfamily contacts by family members outside the family context. Outside of these highly modernized contexts, however, such ill-used concepts prevent one from gaining even a semblance of understanding of the economic aspects of behavior. Outside of a highly modernized context—certainly for most human beings who have ever lived—nearly all actions take place in some family context. This means that economic allocation—from both the production *and* the consumption point of view—has its main locus in family contexts.

Contexts of production have primarily been agrarian for the overwhelming majority of all human beings who have ever lived. But it matters little whether they have been agrarian, hunting and fishing, or a function of animal husbandry, *distribution°*, or craftsmanship. The activities are carried out largely on a family basis in a family context. So, correspondingly, are most of the activities associated with consumption, referring to the preparation and use of food, clothing, shelter, and so forth. If the construction of shelter is done in a family context, why should it be considered consumption simply because it is not carried out by a specialized building industry? Suffice it to say that if these distinctions are drawn in the usual way, that is, if production is production only when it is carried out in a specialized, organizational context, nearly all production for all human beings (until quite recent times) drops out of the picture.

Apart from some of the usual variants—such as that between hunting and fishing on the one hand and agrarian pursuits on the other—some universal propositions can be asserted. For all peoples, including even the most modernized, most literal production and consumption by human beings as such are carried out in family contexts; at least, more is carried out there than in any other single context. Infants are "produced" in a family context. Even in the most highly modernized contexts wherein individuals may well be operating more often in nonfamily than in family contexts, over the general lifespan they still spend more time in a family context than in any other single one. Because practically everyone spent, say, 85 percent of his or her time in some form of family context prior to modernization, even the above qualification is not necessary.

Not only the conception but also the socialization of all human beings is overwhelmingly carried out in family contexts. None of the cases of so-called *feral children*°— whether Romulus and Remus or Amala and Kamala— has been verified, although there have been cases of infants who have been virtually excluded for considerable periods from interaction with other human beings. Without exception, these individuals are described in terms ordinarily used in connection with animals. For example, they are often said to utter the sounds of "animals" (meaning "other animals"), which simply means they speak no recognizable language that would be expected of normally reared children; they have been taught none. Although it may be true that, in some sense, the basic structure of all languages and the ability to learn them may be questions of "biology" (if that is to be distinguished from socialization), surely there is no extant, verified case of anyone who has learned to speak and to understand a language without social interaction in a family, or simulated family, context. Futurists may discuss the possibility of the production of human beings *ex utero* and *in vitro,* attended until birth in human hatcheries, but even our fiction writers assume social interaction for those infants after birth. Socialized human beings are a universal product of family contexts.

This production of human beings in family contexts is closely correlated, in fact is simultaneous, with their consumption—an aspect of the same activities differently viewed. The care of infants and children is never (or only pathologically) affectively neutral. Parents—especially mothers, of course—may vary enormously from one social context to another and from one individual to another in their treatment of infants, but the affective interaction cuts both ways. Both the infant and the mother consume as much affective interaction as they produce.[1] Infants will and do respond to such interaction from birth, and so will, and do, those who interact with them.

One may generalize further: In the early production of human beings in family contexts, apart from the generally accepted biology of conception, mothers are overwhelmingly more important, both in the production of the infants *in utero,* of course, and in their initial care and socialization following parturition.[2] It is not even true

1. If affective interaction is not generally viewed as an "economic product," so much the worse for economics. As Fritz Machlup (1962) has shown so well, much of "family production," especially that carried out in family contexts, has usually been ignored by economists and others (see also Levy 1949, pp. 331, 427, 464–65; Levy 1966, pp. 249–50).

2. It seems not a matter of chance that in *Roget's Thesaurus* the term "parturition" appears under the general heading of "production." No one has ever accused Peter Mark Roget, or John Lewis Roget or Samuel Romilly Roget, for that matter, of being a Marxist or otherwise given to undue emphasis on "economic variables."

that fathers and others are generally more important in the provision of the goods and services that make it possible for mothers to produce and socialize infants and children. Save for conception itself, males may be marginal in these forms of production. Such productive asymmetries are not unprecedented in other mammalian species—lions, for example.

As surely as there is a sexual asymmetry in the production of human beings and their socialization in family contexts, sexual asymmetry is also present in the production of direction and control of family units. Ordinarily considered only in political contexts, these activities nevertheless have a clear and critical economic aspect. Ideally at least, males are more active in these forms of production. All known societies have been or are, at least ideally, patriarchal. Family heads are always, save by default, "supposed to be" male. Unlike the production of human beings and their socialization—which remains wildly asymmetrical until some time well into the childhood of family members—the production of coordination and control in a family context is much less one-sided. Although it is true that the family head is always, ideally speaking, a male, this may not be the actual case even when a properly qualified male is available. It is certainly not likely to be the case when the males involved must be absent from the general family context for extended periods, as is true with some fishing folk, for example.

Male power is also mitigated in another, more far-reaching, respect. In general, the coordination and control of the female side of the family context is delegated to some female, most likely the wife (or sister) of the male family head. Ideally, the family head may directly order and control each female and male family member, but in actuality he does not ordinarily do so. *The allocation of political roles in the family context is not nearly so asym-*

*metrical—apart from the general precedence of males over fe-
males—as is the production and socialization of children.*

In one respect, however, male power is, if anything,
more asymmetrical than are the production and initial care
of offspring. Ideally speaking, male precedence is continual and constant. As observed earlier, the female role vis-
à-vis offspring is much more variable after early childhood. In nonmodernized contexts, male children are
brought under male supervision when they are approximately four or five years old. In addition, until modernization began, education for adulthood was segregated on
the basis of sex from, say, age five to fifteen. Schools were
rare and coeducation hardly existed. Some of these people
were concerned about chastity; some were not.

Female family roles in the preparation of food and
clothing, if not also of shelter, are likely to be more far-
reaching than those of males. Although this is obviously
and easily evident with regard to the provision of food
for newborn infants and young children, it is not as easy
to demonstrate this relative to other family members.
Nevertheless, it may be useful as a hypothesis to maintain
the following: *Until quite recently in human history, what
may be described as the production of family income has been
overwhelmingly dependent on the female members of the family.*
That does not change radically until modern times. In
modernized societies, the production roles that generate
the monetary income, which in turn finances most of the
activities of family members, are largely carried out by
male members operating outside a family context. But
even when this is the case, that part of the income that
refers to the production of human beings and to their socialization, the preparation of food, cleaning, and so
forth, is almost exclusively conducted in the family context by the female side of the family—again, especially by
mothers, of course.

Specialized production roles (i.e., those predominantly

oriented toward production) and specialized consumption roles (i.e., those predominantly oriented toward consumption) are always and everywhere differentiated on the basis of sex in some respects (one may even say in respects that are important to the people involved). There are always some differences, both ideally and actually, in how and what males and females produce and consume in family contexts. Children consume and produce in a different manner from that of infants, and adults do so differently from children or infants. It is also true, however, that insofar as these involvements in economic allocation vary as a function of absolute age and nothing else, sooner or later, if one survives long enough, every individual engages in all of them. *Sex roles are always specialized. In addition, one form of this specialization is always economic, just as another specialization is political.*

Whatever else the acquisition of mates may involve, it assuredly involves some allocation of goods and services over and beyond the acquisition of a mate. Marriage bonds nearly always involve extensive economic interdependencies. Dowries constitute an obvious example of this sort of thing, but so do feasting and partying. The acquisition of mates is always accompanied by ritual, which always involves some allocation of goods and services. *Rituals never involve only free goods! Thus, the formation of marriages always involves interfamilial economic interdependencies.* These interdependencies, in turn, do not vary at random to the interfamily solidarities that ideally and/ or actually follow from the establishment of such relationships. Such interdependency is well-nigh universal until modernization sets in; the extent of the interdependencies varies enormously.

In addition to the economic interdependencies that arise as a function of marriage, there are always other sources of such interdependencies. Marriage is a useful illustration because, without the acquisition of mates, there would be no continuity of the species. This is not to claim that such continuity is foreordained or desirable, but only that if continuity is observed to be in effect, then such interdependencies will also be in effect. On the whole, however, until the last century and a half, nearly all human beings have lived highly localized, decentralized, and self-sufficient lives. The general ideal has been that family members produce everything family members need to consume and vice versa, that is, that they be self-sufficient. But, however much desired, such self-sufficiency has never been complete. Moreover, interfamily interdependencies are never solely a function of marriage. Just as there are some basic forms of economic allocation such as the preparation of food and the use of shelter, there are also always some specialized patterns, which cannot exist without the establishment of interdependencies between and among families, at the least. Some goods and services are always produced and consumed in interfamily contexts.

In general social history, the most nearly universal forms of economic specialization have to do with the *distribution°* of "surpluses" and hence with the service of distribution as such. One of the earliest and most highly developed forms of this economic service (or specialization) must have been the *merchant°,* or trader. Individuals thus identified—at least for a portion of their performances— are above all else specialists in distribution. One probably cannot argue that the levels of economic specialization and differentiation, which give rise to terms like "merchant" or "entrepreneur," are universal traits of any society, however often such patterns may exist in fact. Such diverse exchange patterns as those exemplified by the Kula Ring for the Trobriand Islanders (Malinowski 1922, see esp. chap. 3, 81–104; chap. 11, 267–89; chap. 12, 290–333; chap. 14, 350–65; chap. 17, 392–427; and chap. 19, 464–77) prevent describing Kula Ring participants as merchants. But they are certainly involved in interfamilial exchanges of goods and services.

In modern contexts one tends to think of such exchanges in terms of *markets°*. But markets in the usual sense constitute a specific general (though surely not universal) social development. Although some interfamilial exchanges always exist, nearly all such exchanges probably have not taken place on a market basis.

The minimal expectation that some interfamilial forms of economic allocation exist for all people reinforces another expectation that some form of governance, other than one composed of the family systems of particular individuals, will exist for all human beings. *It can be easily shown that income, power, and* prestige° *never, for any peoples, vary at random one to the other. Only rarely does one of them vary independently of another, ideally or actually—even over a restricted range of values.* [3]

Without falling into the *monism°* of economic determinism, one can nevertheless maintain quite tenably that

---

3. For income, power, and prestige to vary independently of one another (i.e., at random to one another) would require that income be irrelevant to power and prestige, that power be irrelevant to income and prestige, and that prestige be irrelevant to income and power. None of these conditions ever obtains. Income, power, and prestige tend to vary directly. There are rare cases in which these factors do not vary directly, or at least not closely. For example, the Brahmans are the most prestigious individuals in India but they are by no means the wealthiest. The rabbis in the East European shtetl held a similar position. High income may be combined with low prestige especially if the former is from illegal or otherwise socially contemned sources. In general, the correlation of income, power, and prestige is not the result of specific, self-conscious engineering (e.g., rational pursuit of class interests), nor is it the result of ideological factors as such. The correlation of income, power, and prestige tends to vary directly with modernization: the more highly modernized a society, the higher the correlation. Any heavy emphasis on social planning will increase this correlation. If one has two equally modernized societies, one "capitalist" and the other "socialist," the coincidence of income, power, and prestige will be higher in the latter because of the higher level of explicit social planning in socialist contexts generally.

the allocation of power and responsibility never varies at random to that of goods and services, if only because allocations of power and responsibility never involve only free goods; no allocations of goods and services are immune to variations in the allocation of power and responsibility.

Thus, the economic and political aspects of a people— their "economy" and their "polity," if you will—never vary independently one of the other. It also follows, therefore, that when the overwhelming proportion of human interaction takes place within family contexts, then the overwhelming proportion of aspects that might be described as "the economy" or "the polity" also takes place in family contexts. This in turn means that human experience has generally left relatively little scope either for nonfamily governance or for economic interdependencies totally outside of family contexts. *In this sense, the histories of most peoples are misleading because they always reveal more about the patterns of "governments" than about the general patterns of the peoples governed.* Only recently in human history have levels of interdependence and the lowered levels of localized family self-sufficiency made possible (if not necessary) increased centralization in general, and centralization as embodied in governmental organizations in particular. Still, histories so written are oversimplified.

For most human beings, therefore, the "government" at hand is family governance, and the economic interdependence at hand is economic interdependence with one's family members. From both economic and political points of view, therefore, solidarities between parents and offspring, as opposed to all others, are the most important and revealing ones, and those relationships are laid down for the offspring in that initial part of their learning curves discussed so often above. Recent findings, some of an extremely grim sort, argue they are laid down for both children and parents. Child abuse, for example, is a pattern of solidarity. Abused children, apparently with high probability, become abusive parents.

There is an important sense in which the influences that determine in detail how individuals will conduct their lives are "produced" for the individual by other individuals within the family context. *One may add to or subtract from that influence, but one is never free of it.* For most of human history, including much of the present, a given individual will do what the father and mother does and will learn how to do it from the father or mother.

For those relationships, however, one's attention is not particularly drawn to parents teaching children how to behave with their own children. Most initial socialization for most individuals must occur in a family context. Most socialization—if it is this that determines how parents treat their own children—is inculcated before individuals become parents. Therefore, in some way we have not even begun to understand, child-rearing patterns must be inculcated during the initial part of an individual's learning curve, that is, during infancy and young childhood. *The most intense training in the treatment of children may therefore prove to be the treatment the child endures.*

It follows further that if parent-infant and parent–young child relationships are the most strategic ones for understanding human conduct, then, in regard to production, mother-infant and mother–young child relationships are more productive than father-infant and father–young child relationships. This will follow if only because so much more of infant and early childhood experience involves a mother than a father—unless, of course, father-time is considered special "quality time." Finally, it also follows that mothers are more productive in the rearing of both males and females. However important role models (presumably male ones) may be judged to be in later experience, females have more to do with the initial formation both of female and male character than do males. Mothers are thus the quintessential role models for all infants. Alas, social scientists, sociobiologists, natural scientists—none of us have discovered anything approaching an elegant explanation, let alone reduction, of why either males or females behave as they do with regard to infant and child care or of the effects of that behavior.

9

Integration and Expression

As defined in the Glossary, "integration" refers to the adjustments individuals make to the organizations to which they belong. These adjustments enable the members to continue to function within those organizational contexts and enable the organizational contexts themselves to be *eufunctional°*, that is, to persist as described within their social settings. As defined in the Glossary, "expression" denotes the type and limits of reaction, symbolic or otherwise, on the part of individuals or sets of individuals to the various phenomena with which they come in contact. Integration refers to how people adjust, if they do adjust; expression focuses attention on their reactions to various stimuli. Much of what has been said in the preceding chapters can be restated from this point of view, but that is hardly necessary.

The most important observation that can be made in this chapter is in exact consonance with the central theme iterated in the four preceding chapters. For the infant or young child, initial learning of both integration and expression is "mother-taught" insofar as the acquisition or development of these behaviors has any social component. Many elements of both integration and expression are learned or acquired later in life under quite different patterns of interaction with other human beings. But it is exceedingly unlikely—at least that is the hypothesis here—that this subsequent learning varies at random to the patterns of integration and expression laid down initially for infants and young children.

Education is the process whereby the new members of a social system are taught (and learn) its structures or patterns, as well as elements of cognition, data, *aesthetics°*—anything that can be stored in a memory. Because none of what is thought of or defined as social has been elegantly reduced biologically, it is the hypothesis here that this "teaching" is social as well, that all education for humans is in some sense social—also, socialization can be viewed as education. During the initial period of life nearly all teaching is done by mothers. Language itself is one of the most dramatic lessons of this sort. Some learning, however, is inculcated long before an individual develops command of a language.

Perhaps one of the first things an individual learns is the social expression of affective reactions. How much of the expression of affect is learned and how much, in a narrower sense, is puristically biological is not known in any precise sense. Certain things are known, or at least most think they know them. Any newborn infant will sooner or later cry, with or without social interaction. It would not seem farfetched to expect an elegant biological explanation, as well as a social one, for why new mothers, if given the opportunity, will in general fondle and nurture offspring. Correspondingly, the offspring will respond in some fashion. Perhaps some day precise elegant biological explanations will be proffered for this behavior. In any event, the details of what is taught by such interactions may, for the present, be assumed to be social and, at first, largely dependent functions of the action of mothers.

In some cases, the behavior of neonates is mediated by fathers, but one cannot at present construct an argument to the effect that this is always and inevitably the case—especially not in the earlier stages of infancy. Interaction with a mother is, however, certain for all known societies at all periods of time. It may be posited that one of the infant's first bits of such learning is the use of the *generalized negative*°—that is, to reject and later to say "No!" or its equivalent—before learning to accept or to say "Yes!" (or its equivalent) intelligently.

Any infant may be assumed to have certain internal states, crudely illustrated, for example, as hunger, wetness, cold, and so forth. It is assumed here, for puristically biological reasons, that if any of these states are continued long enough they will result in reactions by the infant, for example, kicking, hand-waving, or crying. If any state persists, the infant will cry, and if left completely untended, the infant will die. It is also assumed for these purposes that an infant has a capacity for *memory*° but nothing substantive stored there at birth. For it to be otherwise would seem mystical. It is also assumed that someone in the environment will respond to an infant's reactions, especially crying, by feeding, changing, or warming her or him—or the infant will die.

If the parent, most likely the mother, does not always immediately satisfy the infant, there is the opportunity for something to be stored in the infant's memory. Of the various responses of the infant, crying is the most likely one to be selected and learned as effective. For physiological reasons, if any of these internal states continues long enough without being damped down, the infant will cry. Crying, in addition, can be perceived when other outputs such as kicking or waving of arms or facial contortions cannot.

If not *the* first learning of an infant, one of the first is how to reject successfully, which an infant can accomplish simply by continuing to cry until satisfied. Crying, whatever else it may be, is an infant's first command of the generalized negative. An infant cannot select substantively in early life because little is stored in the memory and the *means*° of expressing whatever is stored are strictly limited. The newborn, if cold, cannot tell the parent that a blanket is what is required when a breast is what is offered. But an infant can continue to cry. One of the first things (if not *the* first thing) all infants learn is how to cry efficiently, and that primal learning involves social interaction with a mother (Kochen and Levy 1956).[1]

The use of the generalized negative expressed especially by crying may influence behavior long after the individual has been socialized in such a way that she or he does not cry save under quite well defined circumstances, as is true to some extent in all social contexts. One may speculate that whenever one reaches the limits of cognition, with or without other social interaction, exploration leading to further cognition (in this case, new cognition as far as the individual is concerned) takes place via the use of the generalized negative, though not necessarily by crying. The utility of the generalized negative would be as true regarding aesthetic creativity as regarding purely cognitive or intellectual creativity; it may have something to do with the general sense that science and art have something in common.

Another vital element in integration has to do with motivation. Again, insofar as the ends of action are not yet explicable on puristically biological grounds, motivation is initially learned from one's mother. For example,

---

1. There is no generalized affirmative. To use the affirmative intelligently, one must understand substantively what the question or the problem means. If, however, there is interaction with an element of the infant's environment, say a mother, who keeps offering alternatives when the infant cries or by other means rejects, then the infant can select by rejection. The infant continues to reject until the "right" response is given. For many, if not all, of these internal states (e.g., hunger), if the "right" response is not forthcoming, the infant will die. Infants will learn if mothers or others keep trying and are not always right the first time. There is a place for ignorance. It may be speculated that if mothers knew everything and were motivated to use their knowledge at once, infants would "learn" nothing.

even if the sociobiologists succeed in producing an elegant puristically biological reduction that proves sexual experience is an end for humans, patterns of sexuality will nevertheless retain a socially learned element. Eating, walking, sexual behavior, and so forth, are all biological in some senses, but members of every society eat, walk, and express themselves sexually in ways that have a socially explicable component. Even breathing and eructation, as variously practiced in different social contexts, contain socially explicable elements—at least for the present. Insofar as these practices are inculcated on infants and young children, they are likely to be inculcated by the individual's mother.

And so it is with motivation. Initially, all infants and young children are taught motivation by their mothers. Insofar as this motivation has to do with ultimate ends and nonempiricals (and to some extent it always does), initial religious patterns are learned from one's mother. Religion in this sense may or may not be the "opiate of the people," but even the expression of such a belief only leads to a social situation in which what appears to be an antireligious, as opposed to an areligious, position becomes in and of itself a religious position. *The important generalization is that religion, too, is initially mother-taught.*

In the preceding chapter on economic allocation, the relevance of mothers with regard to motivation to *intermediate ends*° is touched on sufficiently. The initial inculcation on infants and young children of both ultimate and intermediate ends never varies at random to subsequent acquisition of learning of new and different ultimate and intermediate ends. Insofar as role models are critical to the instilling of motivation, again, *the initial role model of all human beings is a mother.* To the extent that the motivation of males and females is socially learned and differentiated (and for the present it always appears to be), *it is a testament to the remarkable flexibility of mothers that, as role*

*models in some basic sense, they initially inculcate these motiva-
tional differences on the female infants and male infants alike.*

Most of what has been said thus far has described integration to what may be called *certainty situations°*. One ed-
ucates for an expected state of affairs even if one expects
it to change; one *motivates* for an expected state of affairs.
But *uncertainty situations°* always exist for all human beings, though uncertainty may be exponentially increased
in modernized social contexts. Uncertainties have always
abounded with regard to sustenance, security, weather,
and so on. All individuals in all societies have to some extent learned to integrate their behavior to situations of
uncertainty. *Magic°, faddism°*, and other social behaviors
are forms of integration vis-à-vis such situations. All individuals have learned some such adjustments by the time
they reach the age of three, four, or five. And such learning is as surely mother-taught as is almost every other bit
of early socialization.

With the development these days of highly specialized
social contexts, one speaks blithely of "completely different social contexts." But there are no such things. *One
constant of all social contexts is that they all involve individuals
born of, and initially socialized by, women.* This common
element of all humanity is always recognized in some
sense no matter how exotic the differences may be. From
shortly after birth there are no tabula rasa individuals, and
there are no tabula rasa societies. *Cultural (or social) relativity has its limits. The asymmetry of the influence of women on
all infants and children does not vary at random to those limits.*

It is hard to imagine anything more fundamental to expression than language and/or the use of the generalized
negative. Insofar as a social element is present in both,
both are initially inculcated on all individuals by their
mothers. When one thinks of expression, however, one is
quite often preoccupied with affective expression. Affect
is expressed in many different ways, not only as among

different societies but also as regards different contexts within a single society. Insofar as patterns of affective expression are socially inculcated during the first three, four, or five years of life (and some always are), they too are inculcated on all individuals by their mothers. Once again it is important to emphasize that there is a sex-role differentiation in the appropriate patterns of affective expression, as in so many other contexts, and that those patterns are inculcated from birth. Again, *regardless of sex, the individual initially learns socially appropriate patterns of affective expression from her or his mother.*

A principal distinction of affective expression is whether one is expected to repress an expression or to display affects openly. This, too, is highly likely to be differentiated sexually. Nevertheless, *the initial patterns of affective display, inhibited or uninhibited, are mother-taught.* Not the least of these teachings concerns the affective expressions considered appropriate for individuals of different ages. Insofar as there are class differentials, these too are to some degree inculcated at an early age and mother-taught. One initially learns to some extent which and what are appropriately particularistic, affective expressions and which and what are appropriately universalistic ones. Until recently, of course, universalistic expressions were relatively rare in social history.

Finally, recreational and aesthetic forms of expression are also initially mother-taught. All individuals learn to distinguish between the general patterns of ordinary life and *games°*, for example. For some people, recreational patterns are simultaneously combined with the usual duties and concerns of everyday life, and for others they are highly separated and differentiated. For still others, recreation may be very much a matter of *vicarious participation°*, which is an especially noticeable phenomenon in relatively modernized contexts. Whatever the appropriate patterns, they are part of infant and early-childhood learning and, hence, are largely inculcated initially by mothers.

The structures (or patterns) of integration and expression are not less relevant than those of role differentiation, solidarity, political allocation, and economic allocation. They are merely different ways of looking at the same behavior patterns. *None varies from the other in terms of whether they were maternally inculcated in infancy or early childhood as long as the asymmetry of maternal attention to infants and young children persists.* The structures of integration and expression merely highlight the relevance of this inculcation for the continued existence of the above patterns—regardless of whether that persistence be judged desirable or undesirable.

10

Relationships

INTRODUCTION

Relationships are the "elementary particles" of societies; all social systems consist of some set (or sets) of relationships. Families, of course, constitute a specific subset of all relationships. For these purposes, a taxonomy of the most general (basic) aspects of relationships may be stated along six dimensions: First, the cognitive aspect of a relationship refers to what sort of memory and analysis are involved. Second, the membership-criteria aspect refers to who is considered eligible for membership in the relationship, to how the members are chosen. Third, substantive-definition aspect refers to the activities, considerations, rights and obligations, or performances covered by a relationship. Fourth, affective aspect refers to the emotional, or "feeling," aspect of a relationship. Fifth, goal-orientation aspect refers to the motivational aspect of a relationship. Finally, the stratification aspect refers to hierarchical patterns, or their absence, in a relationship.

A relationship is a concrete structure that may involve as few as two individuals or as many as a large finite number. All membership units are examples of relationships. That is to say, all concrete structures are sets of relationships that may range from a large finite number to a single relationship. A two-person, or dyadic, relationship is the simplest form of a social relationship as far as numbers are concerned. But even dyadic relationships can be complex along other dimensions. For example, a mother-son relationship is dyadic, as is that of a traffic officer and a speeder. Numerically, their memberships are equally simple, but they differ considerably in their nonnumerical complexities. Other things being equal, the mother-son relationship is considerably less simple than the one between the traffic officer and the speeder. It must be borne in mind, however, that from a scientific point of view the complexity of a relationship, or even its interest, is a function of the analyst's *conceptual scheme°*. In any event, the common sense that informs us that a mother-son relationship is much more complex and relevant for social analysis than that of a police officer and a speeder will hold for all comparable cases in all known societies. The mother-son dyad is a much more Strategic Research Site than the other for most purposes.

When one starts to examine a society, or any other large-scale organization, one generally has in mind organizational subsystems—that is, concrete substructures. Thus, when one examines a society or country, one expects to find families, some form of government, some forms of neighborhood organization, and the like. But, if one were a tabula rasa about organizations, which would be impossible, one could observe and then plot dyadic relationships and presumably arrive at some sense of how these various relationships aggregate. Many relationships are, in fact, dyadic, as in the case of most friendships. They are not necessarily subsystems of any particular larger organization, except, at some limit, of a society. Societies may be thought of in general as "envelope curves" of social organizations. Friendships often exist as relatively independent subsystems of a society.

Relationships are the building blocks of organizations in general, just as individuals are the members of relationships in general. There is a kind of mysticism in insisting *a priori* that a relationship have "emergent" properties that cannot be understood in terms of the individuals who participate in it, or that larger organizations have "emergent" properties that cannot be understood in terms of the relationships that constitute subsystems of the organization. But, for most purposes, when social analysts study organizations larger than a dyadic relationship, they do not seek reductionist explanations in terms of the latter. Similarly, they do not ordinarily seek a reduction of even a dyadic relationship to matters of individual psychology. But the argument as to whether those reductions can or cannot be made in principle is a meta-argument, not a scientific one. There is no scientific answer other than the present lack of a legitimate elegant scientific reduction.

The analysis of relationships in this chapter aims at an extremely general level of analysis in two senses: First, I will use a set of concepts considered relevant to any relationship, whether dyadic or larger, and, second, I will try to confine my discussion to those relationships, and statements about them, that are regarded as relevant for any society or *world system*°.[1]

The analysis is broken down into some of the most general possibilities in terms of the six aspects set forth

---

1. Perhaps one should be careful about the distinction between societies and world systems. There may well exist a situation today for which levels of interdependency on the planet are so high that the concept of separate societies is no longer useful. The most general system referent may be a world system. Certainly there have existed societies whose members lived in such isolation and at such low levels of interdependency with the members of other societies that they cannot be said to belong to a world system, unless one defines such a system as any set of social systems located on a particular geographical site, in this case, the planet Earth. If, therefore, one is considering any social action or any social systems, regardless of the time referent, the concept of society is more general than that of a world system, however obsolete the concept of separate societies may have become in this century. If the level of interdependency of the planet has rendered the concept of separate societies on earth no longer useful, the world system *is* the only society on earth. Even so, clearly, although that world

at the beginning of this chapter. I then focus more specifically on particular relationships encountered in any society. Before discussing the individual aspects in any detail, I will break down each one into polar terms. *These terms are not conceived as binary distinctions but as polar terms with the possibility of indefinite variations between them.* The polar terms are defined in the Glossary, but for reasons of convenience are discussed here in a somewhat looser fashion. A notational system is also set up for shorthand reference.

The polar terms for cognitive aspects are rational and arational.[2] Membership criteria vary between the poles of universalism and particularism, for which there are three subcategories: *germane particularism°, capricious particularism°,* and *ultimate particularism°.* The simple term "particularism" will suffice for most purposes here. Substantive definition is polarized into *functionally specific°* and *functionally diffuse°,* and the affective aspects vary between avoidant and intimate poles. Goal orientation varies between the poles of *individualistic°* and *responsible°.* Stratification aspects vary between hierarchical and *nonhierarchical°* poles.[3]

---

system is a society, not all societies are (or have been) world systems or parts of world systems.

2. The term *traditional°* may be used instead of *arational* if one wishes, but that term is so encrusted with connotations it is almost impossible to obtain the reader's specific attention to its denotation. Science is a peculiar "language" in that it is the only one for which denotation is everything and connotation is a curse. The term *traditional* will be used, wherever it appears in this work, exactly as defined in the Glossary. In that sense there are *no* traditional, as distinguished from nontraditional, societies. Traditions are part and parcel of *all* societies.

3. All of these terms are defined in the Glossary. Technically, in all cases for which polar terms are involved, a scientist should use relative rather than absolute terms. One should therefore refer to a relationship as "predominantly rational" or "predominantly universalistic," not, ordinarily, as "rational" or "universalistic."

Table 1.   Polar Terms for Relationship Aspects

	x	y
1. Cognitive	rational	arational
2. Membership criteria	universalistic	particularistic
3. Substantive definition	functionally specific	functionally diffuse
4. Affective	avoidant	intimate
5. Goal orientation	individualistic	responsible
6. Stratification	hierarchical	nonhierarchical

For notational purposes, these aspects are numbered 1 to 6. The designation 'x' is used for one set of polar terms and 'y' for the other set. In this notational system, x_1 will designate rational, y_1 arational, x_2 universalistic, y_2 particularistic, x_3 functionally specific, y_3 functionally diffuse, x_4 avoidant, y_4 intimate, x_5 individualistic, y_5 responsible, x_6 hierarchical, and y_6 nonhierarchical (Table 1).[4]

The distinction between ideal and actual patterns, or structures, is used throughout this treatment of relationship aspects. For example, friendships may be described as, ideally speaking, nonhierarchical (or egalitarian), but they are likely, in actuality, to involve some hierarchical elements. This ideal–actual distinction may strike some as contradictory, but the failure of ideal and actual patterns to coincide perfectly is always evident in any social setting. This general failure is one of the most powerful, highly generalized statements one can make about social phenomena. Its implications are extensive and are also essential for an understanding of most social situations. The failure of ideal and actual patterns to coincide *does not* imply the hypocrisy or irrelevance of ideal patterns.

4. The use of the adverbial prefix "predominantly" is implicit as indicated in the preceding note.

RELATIONSHIP ASPECTS

1. *Cognitive Aspects*

The polar terms "rational" and "arational" refer respectively to relationships for which the cognitive aspects are ideally and/or actually expected to be rational—that is to say, subject to what one might call "scientific criteria." Throughout the history of humankind, some element of *tradition°* can at least be discerned—tradition is the essence of what is referred to here as arational. For purposes of illustration, a relationship in terms of which one is supposed to, or in fact does, give empirically or scientifically verifiable explanations for one's behavior, if challenged, approaches the rational pole; and a relationship wherein precedent or authority is invoked approaches the arational pole. If one person in a relationship were to ask the other: "Why do we boil an egg for a given amount of time at sea level and for longer as we climb the mountain?", expecting the explanation to include references to the effect of differing altitudes on the boiling point of water, the relationship is at the rational pole. If the phenomenon is explained thus: "We've always done it that way. That's what our forefathers tell us to do," or the like, the relationship is closer to the arational pole. Two considerations should be kept in mind: Pure rationality may, on the whole, be rare, but the essence of the matter here is (1) *whether* the emphasis tends toward rationality and (2) *how much* emphasis is placed on it.

Some honor Levy-Bruhl[5] because he made one of the

5. In so "honoring" Levy-Bruhl, one may in fact do him an injustice. The classic references for this aspect of his work were published in 1926 and 1935. Levy-Bruhl's statements led to his being attacked by some of the most distinguished social analysts of his day, among them E. Durkheim, M. Mauss, E. E. Evans-Pritchard, and B. K. Malinowski. As in the case of many social scientists, one does Levy-Bruhl greater honor if one accepts him in a vulgar but clear form, that is, as believing that the "primitive mentality" is different in kind from that

great errors in social analysis. Impressed no doubt with the easy dividing line as between literate and nonliterate people, he drew a similar line between rational (logical) and prerational (prelogical) people. Presumably, there were peoples who were incapable of rational action, although there is no evidence that any such peoples ever existed, and certainly none that any do exist. All peoples can make cause-and-effect connections; all peoples can demonstrate their ability to reason logically.

In analyzing social relationships, it is critical to keep in mind that even when the parties to a relationship cite traditional justifications for what they do, *it does not follow* that what they do is irrational given the means at their disposal. Farmers in eighteenth-century China may have farmed as they did largely for traditional reasons, but these reasons coincided to a high degree with what was rational given the means at their disposal. Thus, when one speaks of relationships as predominantly traditional or arational, it by no means follows that action in terms of such relationships is in fact irrational. *Such action often precisely coincides with what is rational given the means at the disposal of the individuals concerned.*

Even when there is a traditional-rational coincidence, the emphasis on arationality (as opposed to rationality) has important implications. For example, if the farmers' resources change markedly, the process of adjustment

---

of people living in terms of modern occidental civilization. By all accounts he sometimes seems to say that there is a clear-cut difference in kind. At other times he seems to fall back on saying that he is describing main lines of difference. There is much more to learn from the vulgar, simple interpretation than from the other. The vulgar form can be definitively disproved and laid to rest forever. And so, one hopes, it has been. However justified one may be in thinking in terms of the vulgar form of Levy-Bruhl's contribution, Jean Cazeneuve (1968) is clearly of the opinion that "Levy-Bruhl himself was on the point of giving it up, as may be seen in his posthumously published notebooks" (p. 265).

will be quite different if the farming methods have been justified on predominantly arational grounds. An adaptation to new means is complicated in such cases by the need to "overthrow" the tradition if an adaptation to the new means is to take place.

There are two fundamental propositions about the cognitive aspects of any relationship. First, nearly all relationships in social history have been predominantly arational. Second, even when great emphasis has been placed on predominantly rational relationships, those relationships have been specific developments in a general social context of predominantly arational relationships. Members of modernized societies generally place great emphasis on predominantly rational relationships, but those emphases have by no means eliminated relationships that are predominantly arational. Social scientists commit the *fallacy of misplaced dichotomies*° by describing relatively modernized societies as "rational." They know not how they mislead!

Kinship relationships in general and family relationships in particular, for example, are always predominantly arational, and virtually all initial learning for all individuals is laid down in the contexts of these relationships. One can imagine, at least in theory, societies for which no predominantly rational relationships are institutionalized—though keep in mind that this does not mean that rational action by members of the society does not exist. *Conversely, societies wherein predominantly arational relationships have not been institutionalized do not exist.*

Predominantly arational relationships are therefore, from the cognitive point of view, the basic form of human relationships. Relationships that are predominantly rational are overwhelmingly likely to be specialized, although for some social contexts (e.g., for many relatively modernized ones) some predominantly rational relationships may be basic. Even for the most highly modernized societies whose members at some time in the life cycle are

all expected to have many predominantly rational relationships, there are still some members of the society
who are not expected to have any. This is patently true of
infants, and almost certainly holds true for most of early
childhood. *In this sense, predominantly arational relationships
are basic, and predominantly rational relationships are specialized when they crop up.*

In the first part of this volume, the universality of the
family and family universals were discussed as basic to
human experience. It follows, therefore, that the family
in general and family universals in particular play a special role in cognitive development. For all known societies—one cannot repeat it too often—infants learn to
walk, talk, eat, sleep, control bodily functions, interact
with other human beings, and behave as females or males
in socially acceptable ways initially in some sort of family
context. The initial part of every human being's learning
curve is lived out in some sort of family context.

However little is known about the physiology of the
brain and how it stores material, initial storage for all human beings takes place in a family context, which is always predominantly arational. This is not to imply that
no rational action takes place in family contexts or that
hardly any action coincides with rational action given the
empirical means-ends of the individuals concerned. For
example, throughout most of human history, it has in
fact been rational for mothers to nurse their infants if they
wanted them to survive. That need not imply that they
have done it for predominantly rational reasons. Again,
what is done for arational or traditional, or even perhaps
for purely physiological, reasons frequently coincides
with what it is rational to do given the means at the disposal of the actors. Even when rationally justifiable action
is in fact arational, it does not imply that the mothers are
unaware of the relevance of these means for this end.

This, in turn, must mean that insofar as "thinking" is
learned by social interaction—regardless of whether one

is speaking of Lapps or Lithuanians, of Christians or Buddhists, of peoples five thousand years ago or of peoples today—*all individuals have been taught to think initially by females.* It might be noted that insofar as one may speak of mammalian species in general "learning to think" by social interaction, all mammals have overwhelmingly learned to think from the females of their respective species.[6] One would be on less certain ground to say all mammals (other than Homo sapiens) learn to think on predominantly arational grounds. All human beings certainly seem to have learned to think that way, or at least they learn to think in terms of a predominantly arational set of relationships.

But even when predominantly arational relationships provide the context of learning, human infants always are taught (and learn) to distinguish rational and arational cognition. One infers this from the fact that all people are able to recognize irrational action or "errors." Irrational action, or error, is something that anyone can do when attempting to behave rationally but failing for some reason to do so. Everyone, similarly, can also distinguish rational and irrational action from arational action, as witnessed by the universal presence of magic and religion. *No one can be rationally irrational (or arational), although one can, of course, rationally attempt to give the appearance of irrationality (or arationality).* Even in the context of magic, as Malinowski (1948, esp. pp. 1–18) pointed out long ago, the most devout believers in magic never confuse "bad" workmanship with "bad" magic.

All peoples learn to distinguish rational, irrational, and arational action, though they may not have a special vo-

6. Individual New World Primates who are born as twins may be an exception to this. When twins exist in some of these species, if both survive, one twin or both are likely to be carried about and handled to a great extent by males except, of course, in the nursing process (Hrdy 1981, pp. 40–41).

cabulary for such distinctions. One may rule out any special hypothesis à la Levy-Bruhl about the very young.
Only the youngest of infants, and those for only a short
time, can be held incapable of rational or *nonrational*°
thinking. Even that may be false. If thinking rationally is
not inherent from birth and if there is any social element
in learning to think rationally and arationally and to distinguish both from irrational thinking, then that too is
learned in a family context and overwhelmingly taught
by mothers.[7]

All that has here been said about the cognitive aspect of
any relationship is entirely independent of the substantive
content of that cognition. The entire subject of substantive commonality of cognition is a strangely neglected
one. Part of it is obvious enough: All human beings with
normal capacities learn to use a language, and all languages have some elements in common. All human beings learn about sensory perceptions; all learn to make
spatial and temporal distinctions, distinctions of color,
magnitude, and so forth, but not a great deal is known
about this. I suggest in chapter 9 that all human beings
initially learn to think by mastering the generalized negative, that there is no such thing as the generalized
affirmative, and that they learn the former in interaction
with their mothers (see pp. 125–27).

Other things being equal, all human beings learn to
think in socially acceptable fashions from females who are
usually their mothers. If they are not the biological mothers, they are usually *in loco matris*. This alone is enough to
make the case for the fact that *initially all cognition for all
human beings is in some sense family-formed and mother-
taught.* One may add to this that the other influential ac-

7. So much for any hypothesis à la Levy–Bruhl to the effect that females cannot think rationally! *Consciously or unconsciously, females initially teach rational thinking to all people.*

tors in an infant's cognitive formation are likely to be members of an infant's own family. This in turn follows from the fact that, until quite modern times, more than 85 percent of all people who ever lived probably spent more than 85 percent of all of their waking and sleeping hours within eyeshot and/or earshot of other members of their own families. This figure could quite tenably be as high as 99.9 percent in the case of infants. The presence of nonfamily members, and hence their relevance, undoubtedly varies according to the patterns of interaction among family members and nonfamily members; some such interaction, of course, always exists. In modernized social contexts, individuals spend less time in a family context, but the difference is not so great in the case of infants as in the case of others.

The fact that initial cognition for infants is family-formed points directly to the following: For all known societies, the institutionalized form of the cognitive aspects of family relationships is predominantly arational. The literatures, or their equivalent—myths, tales, lore, and so forth—of many societies are lost or unknown. Wherever there is a literature or body of myths, puristically rational attitudes (i.e., a purely instrumental approach) toward family relationships is marked wicked. *Family relationships everywhere and at all times are, and have been, institutionalized as predominantly arational, as being in at least some sense closely related to the sacred.* It would therefore seem to follow that all initial learning about relationships involves a predominantly arational relationship as an ideal pattern.

There will be no departure from this universal pattern unless one invents a totally nonfamilial set of relationships for the socialization of infants—a set that is itself a set of predominantly rational relationships. Empirically speaking, nothing seems less likely. It is difficult to imagine what such a pattern might be.

This matter may be pushed yet a bit further. It is quite possible that many societies and social settings have been characterized only by relationships institutionalized as predominantly arational. Until relatively modernized societies developed, the ratio of relationships institutionalized as predominantly arational to those institutionalized as predominantly rational has been high. Even when that ratio begins to shift, one may doubt whether the denominator ever exceeds the numerator—even if it does in a numerical sense, it would not affect its significance for initial cognitive experience or as regards the effective significance of the relationship contexts in which the ratio occurs. *Relationships institutionalized as predominantly rational occur within a context of relationships institutionalized as predominantly arational. One learns about these relationships initially from one's mother—even in the most highly modernized social settings.*

Moreover, it can be maintained that *the longer a given relationship actually continues—no matter how thoroughly it is institutionalized as predominantly rational—the more likely it will come to include nonrational elements in general and arational ones in particular.* In a trivial sense, the more a relationship perdures, the greater is the probability of *error* in terms of it—that is, the more likely it will contain irrational elements. Importantly for analysis, however, the longer a relationship exists, the greater is the probability that some normative elements not within the original "specifications" will obtrude—a more personal relationship, whether positively or negatively evaluated, develops. Other things being equal, the more personal a relationship, the more difficult it is to approach rational behavior in terms of it. *Predominantly arational behavior, on the other hand, does not tend to break down in the direction of predominantly rational behavior.* If predominantly arational behavior breaks down, it does so in the direction of an alternative form of arational emphasis.

2. Membership-Criteria Aspects

The two polar terms for membership criteria, "universalism" and "particularism," are further amplified by distinguishing three forms of the latter. The selection of members for a universalistic relationship involves no social barring, *and* the selection criteria are germane to the purpose(s) of the relationship. Any taint of social barring or of nongermaneness moves the relationship toward the other pole. The relationship is germanely particularistic if social barring is combined with germaneness; it is capriciously particularistic if no social barring is involved but the criteria are not germane; and it is ultimately particularistic if both social barring and nongermaneness are involved.

For example, election to Phi Beta Kappa is ideally purely universalistic and is actually predominantly universalistic. There may be some particularistic criteria that affect entrance to, say, Harvard College, but within the set of people admitted, great care is taken that neither social barring nor capricious characteristics enter the selection for membership in Phi Beta Kappa there. In actuality, there are probably some particularistic elements both in admission to Harvard and in selection for Phi Beta Kappa after one is admitted. Undoubtedly, however, the predominant emphasis is on universalistic criteria, ideally speaking; actually speaking, particularistic criteria probably play quite a small role. After all, some of the students who are admitted to Harvard in part for particularistic reasons could have gotten in even without particularistic help.

Succession to the throne of England is germanely particularistic both ideally and actually. At any given time, only a single individual, and that one related to the previous king or queen by kinship and importantly, but somewhat less importantly, qualified by sex as well, is eligible to succeed to the throne of England. Social barring is certainly involved there, but capriciousness is not. An important part of the relationship of the sovereign to his or her subjects is the continuity of that kinship line and all the symbolism that goes with it. Thus, the social barring involved is germane to the purposes of the relationship, and, therefore, it may be described as predominantly germanely particularistic, both ideally and actually.

A preference for red-headed, green-eyed, freckled female secretaries is overwhelmingly likely to be capriciously particularistic both ideally and actually. The job description of a secretary is capable of variation. Given the usual ones, however, characteristics of red hair, green eyes, freckles, and femaleness, although they involve no social barring, are certainly not germane. Such criteria might be germane, even highly universalistic, for certain types of roles in color movies, television, or for the stage.

Racism°, as that term is ordinarily used, is ultimately particularistic. Discrimination against people on the basis of *race°* certainly does involve social barring. The definitions of socially distinguished races are always closely related to kinship-descent criteria. Races, moreover, are socially defined rather than puristically biologically defined—beliefs of the racists to the contrary notwithstanding. Racist criteria are also capricious regarding matters that involve eligibility for jobs, voting, housing, and so forth. Bigotry may be considered germane only by positing that it is somehow good for the bigoted and that their good is a good.[8]

---

8. Capricious and ultimate particularism have increased implications for the operation of the general systems of which they are a part in modernized contexts, where the emphases on universalism always become high by contrast with relatively nonmodernized contexts in general. In relatively nonmodernized contexts, there is not a great deal of leeway for predominantly capricious particularism to operate, and interdependencies are sufficiently low so that the capricious particularism of a given relationship is not likely to interfere with much else. In

Of primary concern here is the distinction between predominantly universalistic and particularistic relationships without reference to distinctions on lower levels of generality. *The basic form of all human relationships is predominantly particularistic. Predominantly universalistic relationships, when institutionalized, always involve some element of specialization.* As in the case of cognitive aspects, when predominantly universalistic criteria are institutionalized, this always happens in a general social setting of predominantly particularistic relationships. This continues to hold true even in the most highly modernized contexts, although there may be some question about this in strictly numerical terms. *Even in modernized contexts, however, the intensity of the predominantly particularistic relationships is much greater than the intensity of the predominantly universalistic ones.*

It is beyond question that, for all known societies, initial socialization of the individual takes place in terms of predominantly particularistic relationships. This will follow, as the night the day, from the fact that for all peoples, including the most highly modernized, initial socialization is overwhelmingly likely to take place in some sort of family context. Thus, as with the cognitive aspects of relationships, initial learning about relationships is about predominantly particularistic ones. In some sense, *members of any society, including the most highly modernized ones, originally learn predominantly universalistically institutionalized relationships as some sort of departure from "normal," that is, predominantly particularistically institution-*

---

relatively nonmodernized contexts, it is also true that predominantly ultimately particularistic relationships differ from kinship relationships only in the capriciousness of the relationship. The implications of that for other areas are likely to be subsumed under the normal range of kinship dyscrasias. Moreover, and most obviously, in relatively modernized contexts, comparatively small differences in germane abilities may have far-reaching implications for productivity.

alized relationships. Predominantly universalistic relationships are, in a sense, regarded as "inhuman." In much of
fundamentalistic reaction° against modernized patterns, the
"inhumanity" of predominantly universalistic relationships is often one aspect of modernization being rejected.

The overwhelming basis for particularism in social relationships in all societies is kinship in general and the
family in particular. The basic form of all particularism is
nepotism; indeed, that specific kinship term is often used
among modern peoples as a synonym for any form of
particularism. One would expect this because most individuals have spent the vast majority of their time on this
earth in some sort of family context, and even the most
modern have received most of their initial learning in
family contexts. For all peoples at all times, the initial
identification of *who* an individual is has been, and continues to be, established on the basis of kinship in general
and the family in particular.

*For most of history and in most social settings, the most basic
form of particularism has been "germane" particularism.* It is
"germane" because, for most individuals in world history
(certainly for nearly all nonmodernized people), the basic
form of organization for nearly all purposes is some form
of family or kinship organization. Therefore, in this
sense, kinship criteria in general and family criteria in
particular are germane. Ideally speaking, this is no longer
true for many relationships in a relatively modernized
context; it is not even true, ideally speaking, for some relationships in a relatively nonmodernized context. Membership in the Chinese imperial bureaucracy is a clear-cut
case of the latter, and examples in a modernized context
are myriad and well known.

As indicated above, much arational action coincides
with what would be rational given the means at the disposal of the actors. *Predominantly germane particularistic action may not be widely at variance with predominantly univer-*

salistic action. Such coincidences are general for humans and probably enable any subsequent institutionalization of predominantly rational and universalistic relationships.

Other things being equal—as noted above in connection with the cognitive aspects—the longer predominantly rational relationships are continued, the more likely that the emphasis will shift in favor of arational elements. So correspondingly, *the longer any predominantly universalistic relationship persists, the greater is the probability that it will assume characteristics of a predominantly particularistic one.* As noted in other connections, although the terms are polar terms, one pole is always more unstable than the other at the most general level. *When and if predominantly particularistic relationships break down, they do so in the direction of other particularistic forms, not in the direction of universalism.*

Although this study emphasizes the social patterns common to all human beings—that is, common patterns that are not adequately explicable in terms of human heredity and the nonhuman environment—a quite significant difference between relatively modernized and relatively nonmodernized contexts arises in connection with the membership-criteria aspect of relationships. For predominantly particularistic relationships to be in force, one must have a basis for knowing who any given individual is. Prior to the development of relatively modernized contexts, the vast majority of all individuals know the individuals with whom they interact; controlling for relative ages, they know one another from birth, or at least from very early childhood. Most of the people one knows are likely to be family members or other kin. The others, although not kin, are usually well known to the individuals concerned. They are likely to be neighbors. Life for most relatively nonmodernized people is lived out on a highly localized, self-sufficient basis. One is therefore likely to know exactly who an individual is. As a consequence, a generalized, residual category of *strangers°* constitutes a relative unknown.

In relatively nonmodernized contexts the great majority of individuals encounter few strangers. Thus, in an anomalous sense, even a stranger is identified by who he or she is. An individual can be excluded from a relationship specifically because she or he is a stranger. "Stranger" is a germane identification. As soon as one moves into relatively modernized contexts, however, fleeting, casual contacts with strangers are taken for granted. One has so many relationships with strangers that identification of someone as a stranger usually can no longer serve as a germane form of particularism one way or the other.

For relationships institutionalized as predominantly universalistic, the categorization of an individual as a stranger is not sufficient. Perhaps no one is socially barred from being so categorized, but the mere fact of being a stranger is not germane to the purposes of most relationships. For universalistic relationships it is required that the individual not be socially barred from becoming a member of the relationship on the basis of who he or she is, and that the criteria involved be germane to the purposes of the relationship. In relatively modernized contexts, there is a sense in which one loses all sense of who a stranger is. *Nearly all human beings with whom one interacts in a relatively modernized context are strangers. But, although this is true in a numerical sense, it is certainly not true as far as the strength and intensity of relationships are concerned.* Relationships with strangers in a relatively modernized context are probably characteristically less strong and certainly less intense than relationships with nonstrangers. Fear of strangers, however, can and often does raise the level of intensity.

It cannot be overemphasized that as far as all human beings are concerned—regardless of modernization—the relevance of predominantly particularistic relationships cannot be ignored. This alone is sufficient reason to state that it is always and everywhere absolutely and nonsensically misleading to call highly modernized contexts in general "universalistic." Indeed, taken as a whole, such contexts are not even *predominantly* universalistic in any general sense, although it is true that many relationships in such a context are institutionalized on a predominantly universalistic basis, whereas such institutionalization is relatively rare in nonmodernized contexts.

It is also true that institutionalizations of predominantly universalistic criteria are strategic, especially where factors of technology, productivity, political participation, and the like are involved. Predominantly universalistic relationships, however important they become, never render predominantly particularistic relationships insignificant in understanding the society in general or even in understanding how predominantly universalistic criteria can be institutionalized at all. Finally, it must be iterated that although all people in relatively modernized contexts come to have many predominantly universalistic relationships, these are specialized rather than basic relationships when considered in the context of society as a whole.

It cannot be overemphasized that *the basic human pattern, as far as membership criteria of relationships are concerned, is a predominantly particularistic relationship of some sort.* There may be, and almost certainly have been, peoples for whom no predominantly universalistic relationships are institutionalized. There have not been, are not, and cannot be any peoples for whom no predominantly particularistic relationships are institutionalized. The polar distinction used is not symmetrically institutionalized, and *it is certainly not, in any sense, binary.* The use of the terms *universalistic* to describe the relationships of modernized societies and *particularistic* to describe those of non-

modernized societies (or the corresponding binary distinction between *achievement*° and ascription) constitutes
another instance of the fallacy of misplaced dichotomies.

If one insists on a binary distinction, universalistic relationships could not exist in any context. Kinship in general and the family in particular are always matters of particularism, whatever else they may be. No one, at any
point in her or his life, does anything that is totally without interdependence with, or varies at random to, what
has happened to her or to him in some kinship context—
especially, of course, during infancy and early childhood.
Therefore, some particularistic considerations are relevant to all subsequent, supposedly germane criteria.
There can be no getting away from this unless intelligence, "character," and even fleetness of foot can be
shown to vary at random to an individual's experience in
family and kinship contexts.

Even when the institutionalized form of membership
criteria is predominantly universalistic, its actual form
may be predominantly particularistic. Again, the longer
any given relationship continues, the greater is the likelihood that particularism will prevail. Universalistic criteria always break down in the direction of particularism.
Other things being equal, a ten-year relationship between
a foreman and a worker, in even the most modern context, will contain more particularistic (e.g., personal) elements than one of only a year's duration. The reverse is
not true. If the ideal form of a relationship is predominantly particularistic, the relationship is overwhelmingly
likely to remain so, no matter how long it continues.

All human beings originally learn about particularistic
criteria in a family setting from their mothers. If they
learn about universalistic criteria, such knowledge is always superimposed on their learning about particularistic
ones. That superimposition, too, is almost certainly initially done by mothers.

3. Substantive-Definition Aspects

The polar distinction for the substantive-definition aspects of a relationship is between functional specificity and functional diffuseness. These concepts may vary at random to the actual content of a relationship. This distinction solely concerns whether a relationship is precisely defined and delimited or vaguely defined and delimited. As Talcott Parsons put it long ago in his lectures, the distinction deals with the burden of proof. Does a relationship that is incorporating a new element require the burden of proof to rest on the proponent or on the opponent of inclusion? If the relationship tends toward specificity, the burden of proof falls on the proponent; if predominantly functionally diffuse, the burden of defense falls on the one who wishes to evade the asserted obligation. As originally used by Parsons, and as used here, this too is a polar, not binary, distinction. It is also an asymmetrical distinction. *The basic form of human relationships involves the institutionalization of predominantly functionally diffuse relationships. Functionally specific relationships are always institutionalized within a general social context of functionally diffuse relationships and always represent specialized rather than basic relationships from the point of view of a society as a whole.* Not all predominantly functionally diffuse relationships are basic ones, but no predominantly functionally specific relationships are basic for human beings in general.

As with predominantly rational and universalistic emphases, in highly modernized contexts some predominantly functionally specific emphases become basic in a special sense, just as literacy may be regarded as a form of *basic cognition°* in those contexts, whereas it is not for human beings generally. In relatively modernized contexts, all people (if they live long enough) will sooner or later have some predominantly rational, universalistic, and functionally specific relationships. The particular ones they have are not likely to be common to the set as a whole—although some may be, as in the case of the relationships in educational (e.g., school) and civic (e.g., governmental) contexts.

As one would expect, family and kinship relationships are anywhere and everywhere institutionalized as predominantly functionally diffuse. This is true of the most highly modernized societies as well as the least modernized societies, and it continues to hold true despite all references to marriage and family contracts and the like or to newly created patterns in these contexts. The common building blocks of all family and kinship systems—mother-son, mother-daughter, father-son, father-daughter, husband-wife, sister-sister, sister-brother, brother-brother—are never institutionalized as predominantly functionally specific. The same may be said of any further extensions beyond these universal building blocks. They may be extended through third-generation relationships, avuncular relationships, and so forth. *Ideally speaking, kinship relationships of whatever sort are predominantly functionally diffuse in all known societies.*

Thus, as one would expect, *everyone's initial socialization, as far as the substantive-definition aspects of relationships are concerned, takes place in a functionally diffuse context. Individuals learn about functional specificity, if they learn about it at all, by contrast with functional diffuseness, just as one learns about rationality by contrast with arationality and about universalism by contrast with particularism.* As one would expect from the discussion in the preceding chapters, functional diffuseness is initially learned in a family context from one's mother.[9]

9. While it will follow deterministically or with very high probability that initial learning of rationality, universalism, and functional specificity is maternally inculcated, it does not follow that these three poles are equally emphasized. *Although it can be maintained that some rationality is always taught, and taught by mothers, it cannot equally be main-*

Homo sapiens is a functionally diffuse mammal capable of functional specificity but critically dependent on it only in relatively modernized contexts. Even then, the necessity of functionally specific relationships never eliminates functionally diffuse ones. Again, it is possible that a society exists wherein all social relationships are institutionalized as predominantly functionally diffuse. But there cannot be a society whose members have relationships that are institutionalized, without exception, as functionally specific. Even if the family could be eliminated, the society just hypothesized could not exist, because infants and small children cannot be cared for on a functionally specific basis. Even the Chinese—a relatively nonmodernized people for five thousand years and reluctant to deal with strangers lest they subsequently become responsible for their welfare—held that even a villain could not stand idly by and permit a small child to fall into a well.

The concepts of functional specificity and diffuseness have a long pedigree in social analysis. They crop up again and again in the persistent form of the fallacy of misplaced dichotomies. The distinction is the essence of the Gemeinschaft-Gesellschaft distinction—the distinction between status and contract, and the distinction between folk and urban, mechanical and organic, and so forth, societies. The epitome of all functionally specific relationships is the legal contract which, if perfectly drawn from the points of view of all the contracting members, would perfectly specify all possible rights and obligations of all possible participants for all possible times and places. The perfect contract would perfectly delimit and define all the

---

tained that universalism and functional specificity are always taught even though they are in some sense implicit as polar categories. If they are taught, however, they are almost certainly first taught by mothers to their offspring.

relationships concerned. Of all the great figures in social analysis who dealt in this fallacy of misplaced dichotomies, only Emile Durkheim detected the error and abandoned the distinction in that form.[10]

The important part of Durkheim's realization is that in terms of the distinction utilized here, functionally specific relationships all take place within a setting of diffuse relationships. For history as a whole, the basic form of any relationship is one that is predominantly functionally diffuse. If one insists on setting up the distinction as binary, there would be *no* cases of functionally specific relationships. Even if one sets up the distinction as polar, as is done here, predominantly functionally diffuse relationships are basic to humankind in general. Relationships that tend toward specificity always appear as specialized cases, when they do appear.

Relationships that are functionally specific are institutionalized so frequently in relatively modernized contexts that one tends to take them for granted as normal and

10. Durkheim regarded the contract as the epitome of what he referred to as the "organic" society, by contrast with the "mechanical" one. Unlike other discoverers of this distinction, Durkheim, at his very invention of it, faced the problem of what he termed "the noncontractual elements in contracts." He clearly understood that those noncontractual elements on which the contract system had to rest were exactly the kinds of patterns that he held to be characteristic of mechanical systems. As far as is known, Durkheim never used the distinction after the book in which he made that discovery was published. Except for the early work of Talcott Parsons, the vast majority of, if not all, social scientists who teach the distinction at all treat it as one of Durkheim's great contributions to social analysis. None who have, save for Parsons, teach that Durkheim was the only person who invented the distinction, saw through the distinction, and abandoned the distinction because he knew it could not be a binary, that is, a dichotomous, distinction (Durkheim 1932, esp. pp. 184–87; Parsons 1937, pp. 312–14). I can also report on Parsons's observance of this point about Durkheim from attendance at his lectures over a period of ten years (1937–47), with four years out for World War II.

"natural." They nevertheless possess the same kind of inherent instability that characterizes relationships institutionalized as predominantly rational and universalistic. *The longer any given institutionalized, predominantly functionally specific relationship persists, the more likely it will tend in the direction of diffuseness.* One may precisely define and delimit a relationship that is on the whole fleeting and casual, but it is difficult, if not impossible, to do that with a relationship that persists over twenty or thirty years.

Because the family patterns characteristic of all human beings are predominantly functionally diffuse, and because all of the building blocks of social relationships in the family context—mother-son, father-son, mother-daughter, father-daughter, sister-sister, brother-brother, sister-brother, husband-wife—are institutionalized as such, it follows that the initial learning about relationships for all human beings is about functionally diffuse relationships.

As one grows older, if one learns about predominantly functionally specific relationships at all, one learns about them as contrasted with relationships that are predominantly functionally diffuse. One learns that the former are the kinds of relationships one has with people *who are not members of one's family.* If push comes to shove, they are relationships that tend to be less strong and less intense than the latter—even in the most highly modernized contexts. Even if, ideally, they are not less strong, they are actually likely to be unless most carefully reinforced. Of course, *all humans initially learn about functionally diffuse relationships (and about specific ones, if they learn about them) in a family context from their mothers.*

Functionally specific societies do not exist. Predominantly functionally specific relationships always exist within a general context of relationships that are diffuse. To describe a society as functionally specific is, again, to commit the fallacy of misplaced dichotomies.

Ideally speaking, predominantly functionally specific relationships are, in a sense, cut off from affective involvement—that is, from an individual's emotions or "feelings." It should go without saying that there is an affective aspect of everything any given actor does. But affects are notoriously difficult to define and delimit precisely, even in these days of reliance on "thick description." Individuals display varying degrees of consideration toward others with whom they have relationships, *but it is certainly true that if predominantly functionally specific relationships are to persist as ideal patterns at all (however unstable in the long run), they must be relationships wherein members regard one another instrumentally—never as ends in themselves!*

In family contexts specifically and kinship contexts generally, individuals are never considered in a purely instrumental manner. Were family members in general and offspring in particular treated in such a fashion, it would be impossible to rear stable individuals. *It is not even possible for all actors at all times to treat all other adult actors in a purely instrumental fashion.* This renders all purely utilitarian hypotheses problematic. This does not mean that rational utilitarian models are useless in human analysis, any more than the fact that empirical bodies do not fall *in vacuo* on earth means that the formula $s = \frac{1}{2}gt^2$ is irrelevant to earthbound ballistics.

Those reared in a modern setting take relationships that are institutionalized as predominantly functionally specific so much for granted that when social scientists describe whole societies as functionally specific the scientists are taken seriously. The question that should arise is how one ever gets from the appreciation of predominantly functionally diffuse relationships inculcated on all infants to an appreciation and understanding of predominantly functionally specific relationships, either ideally or actually. *Functionally diffuse relationships are a given for hu-*

man beings; but relationships that are functionally specific re-
quire a great deal of explanation. One has to be carefully
taught, and is so taught by one's mother.

Where relationships that are predominantly functionally specific are not institutionalized, they may still exist
by default, but that lack of institutionalization is not
likely to raise serious questions for the members of relatively nonmodernized societies. Thus, in social settings
where predominantly functionally diffuse relationships
alone are institutionalized, members of all social relationships somehow have to juggle family obligations that are
predominantly functionally diffuse with similar obligations to nonfamily members. When functionally specific
relationships are institutionalized, they too must be jug-
gled. Family relationships usually take precedence over
nonfamily ones: They are characterized by both stronger
and more intense solidarities.

This cannot be held to be a universal social trait. It is manifestly not the case in many relatively modernized contexts. Indeed, it is manifestly not the case in many relatively nonmodernized contexts. Relationships with chiefs
and "states" and even with nonfamily kin may take
precedence over (i.e., be stronger than), and in rare cases
even be more intense than, any family relationship. They
may even be predominantly functionally specific. *If such a*
relationship takes precedence over a predominantly functionally
diffuse family relationship, it cannot fail to be functionally dif-
fuse itself, no matter how much specificity is present (cf. pp.
155–58). Thus, the obligation of all citizens to pay an income tax involves a predominantly functionally specific
relationship that takes precedence over family relationships. The income-tax obligation is itself binding because
it is more generally held that the relation of a citizen or a
subject to some system of governance takes precedence
over any family obligations. Thus, it too must contain
some elements of functional diffuseness. The many note-

worthy eighteenth-century attempts (and efforts since then) to make all such matters clear with a written constitution represent spectacular attempts to move governments toward functional specificity. Even here, however, the concept of patriotism is clearly predominantly functionally diffuse. For all the "diffuseness" and flexibility of the U.S. Constitution, its strain toward specificity is particularly clear in contrast to England's unwritten constitution. The U.S. Constitution's strains toward specificity are especially evident in the document's attempt to limit governmental powers.

If functionally diffuse *nonfamily* relationships always require a juggling with functionally diffuse family relationships, the juggling aspect is even more obvious when one considers the interdependency of nonfamily relationships that are institutionalized as predominantly functionally specific with family relationships that are always institutionalized as predominantly functionally diffuse. *Thus, whenever predominantly functionally specific relationships take precedence over family relationships—however socially distant that may seem—they place limits on the strength and intensity of family relationships.* Most of the major tragic themes of all literatures revolve around possible or actual conflicts of more or less functionally diffuse obligations.[11]

11. It might be interesting to speculate on the possibility of functionally diffuse relationships, with or without reference to institutionalization, in other animal species. The most obvious place to look, of course, would be in some family or kinship context, but I for one would duck pushing the search back into the context of the social insects. In most mammalian species, these problems are minimized by two extremely general patterns, the first being the limitation of the time spent together by most mating pairs, and the other being the abandonment or driving out of offspring after they have reached a certain level of maturation. On the other hand, there certainly are mammals like lions and wolves, for example, for whom the mating relationship seems to remain stable over relatively long periods and for whom some of the offspring seem not to be abandoned or driven off. For all such species, there are almost certainly what may be described

Perhaps one further line of speculation about the sub-stantive-definition aspects of any relationship taken in conjunction with what has been said above about particularism is in order. Initial learning for all human beings is laid down by mothers in terms of family-based particularism and family-based functional diffuseness. The family-nonfamily distinction is the basic form in terms of which all humans learn the distinctions between "us" ("we") and "them" ("they") and between "us" ("we") and "you." Furthermore, because the relationships that one initially learns are predominantly functionally diffuse, *there is always a potential conflict between one's relations with any nonfamily member and one's relations with family members.* In terms of functionally diffuse relationships, the burden of proof is on the individual who wishes to give priority to a nonfamily consideration. Peoples may vary as to how they treat outsiders, but no peoples fail to distinguish outsiders. In addition, of course, for nearly all people who lived before "modern times"—and perhaps for many, if not most, people on the planet today—experience with outsiders may have been familiar, but experience with a special set of outsiders, strangers, was and is relatively rare.

4. Affective Aspects

The polar distinction for the affective aspects of any relationship is that between avoidant and intimate affects. The term "affect" leaves much to be desired. Save for its unfamiliarity and hence pauce connotations, it is in no

---

as functionally diffuse relationships, and there must be mechanisms of interrelating these relationships with relationships with other members of the species for whom these patterns are not in force. One tends, of course, to speculate only on social mechanisms for handling these matters, but there may be some puristically biologically explicable ones as well. If such should prove to exist for other mammals, who is to say, *a priori,* that none such exist for Homo sapiens? The sociobiologists may someday learn about such matters.

way more exact than the term "emotion" or the ordinary usage of "feeling." The use of the term "cathexis" adds nothing to the precision of these discussions. In seeking to establish a range of variation with regard to the type of emotional content ideally or actually invested in a relationship, "avoidant" and "intimate," as terms, can apply to any relationship and can also be treated as polar terms. A completely avoidant relationship is completely devoid of affective interaction. There are no such relationships; none are precisely neutral or nonaffective. Humans never act without some affective involvement. A predominantly avoidant relationship emphasizes such affects as respect; the individuals involved treat one another with high levels of *formality°*, and any overt displays of emotion or feeling are minimized. Predominantly intimate relationships are characterized by considerable levels of *informality°* and by open display of affects. What sometimes are thought of as the positive affects (e.g., love) are no more intimate in this sense than are open, uncontrolled displays of hostility.

Terms like "hot-blooded" and "cold-blooded" cut across those lines. Terms like "caring" ordinarily connote, if they do not denote, intimate relationships. For some societies, some family relationships are institutionalized as on the whole avoidant, and yet even they are certainly supposed to be "caring relationships." The father-son relationship in a gentry family in imperial China was likely to be institutionalized as predominantly avoidant, but at the same time both father and son were expected to "care" about one another. The concepts involved in affective aspects are not comfortably developed from a scientific point of view despite all of the increased sophistication brought to us by Freud and others.

One can imagine the existence of societies that are in no way characterized by the institutionalization of predominantly avoidant relationships, though there may be no such cases. *But it is not possible even to imagine a society for which no predominantly intimate relationships are institutionalized.* The family is, of course, the cockpit of intimacy. Examples of predominantly avoidant relationships internal to family structure are not hard to find, but they always exist within a general context of predominantly intimate relationships. There is probably no society whose members are not expected to "feel at home" with the members of their own families. In modernized contexts, the family becomes the "castle of the me." When one does not feel at home in the family context, the implication is that something is awry. Here again the relevance of intimacy to the rearing of infants and children is critical.

Although no elegantly reduced explanations exist for this, human females may be biologically predisposed toward intimate relationships with their offspring if such relationships are permitted, as they almost always are. Exceptions would probably everywhere be regarded as pathological. A similar biologically based hypothesis about biological fathers is more farfetched. There are, one suspects, physiological reasons why a woman with a newborn infant will, given the opportunity, handle it, fondle it, nurse it, and in general display intimate affective involvement.[12] Moreover, although it has never been experimentally proved (who would permit the experiment?), it may be taken here as an axiom that one cannot rear infants and young children on a pure or even highly avoidant basis. A Skinner box can be used only so far. It

---

12. I suspect (think?) that although most mothers learn something, perhaps a lot, about infants from their own mothers, they learn most from having infants, holding them, caring for them, and so forth. Fathers, I suspect (think?), learn most about infants from the mothers with whom they live and from the infants who are themselves learning so intensively from their mothers.

must follow, therefore, that *one learns to sustain predominantly avoidant relationships by contrast with and within a context of having learned to sustain predominantly intimate ones.* Again, everyone initially learns this within a family context and from one's mother. Everywhere and for all peoples, formality is learned within a context of informality: "You mustn't address your father that way!" "You must kowtow to the emperor!"

Although the family may be characterized by some predominantly avoidant relationships, that cannot be the general form of family relationships. The general form must be predominantly intimate. Insofar as predominantly avoidant relationships are institutionalized within a family context, one learns to perform in terms of them as a special departure from ordinary family behavior. Predominantly avoidant relationships involve individuals who are relatively little or only marginally involved in the direct handling and rearing of infants and young children.

When predominantly avoidant relationships are institutionalized in family structure, they probably serve as a sort of bridge in learning how to sustain nonfamily relationships. Other things being equal, nonfamily relationships are much more likely to be avoidant than are family relationships, although, as indicated above, it is not impossible to imagine a society completely lacking predominantly avoidant relationships—ideally speaking.

Furthermore, relationships that are institutionalized as predominantly avoidant have the kind of intrinsic instability that has been discussed above. To wit, *the longer any given predominantly avoidant relationship persists, the greater is the probability that it will change in the direction of a predominantly intimate relationship.* But predominantly intimate relationships have no corresponding tendency to change over time into predominantly avoidant ones—cynicism about marriage notwithstanding.

In reductionist terms, it is easier to conceive of a legitimate and fruitful—even elegant—puristically biological reduction of predominantly intimate social patterns than of predominantly avoidant ones. There is, however, no obvious or well-known attempt to examine the relationships of animals other than Homo sapiens from this point of view.

Within the family context, if predominantly avoidant relationships are institutionalized, they are never generally institutionalized for mother-infant or mother–young child relationships. They are most likely to characterize the relations between father, or family head, and offspring. Predominantly avoidant relationships do not, of course, ordinarily characterize relationships between husbands and wives, although the ethic of the imperial Chinese was clear-cut in this respect: Intimacy was permitted on the marital couch, but avoidance was the ideal apart from that. Needless to say, even for Chinese gentry families, such avoidance was probably rarely maintained even by the "superior man."

The line of speculation stretches out from here. Granted, one cannot prove that in all known social settings, some predominantly avoidant relationships are institutionalized. One might guess that some such always are institutionalized, and certainly some such are institutionalized for any societies or social settings on which we have any considerable amount of information. One can maintain that this kind of distinction is not entirely foreign to other mammalian species that have something at least intuitively analogous to family systems. When, and if, predominantly avoidant relationships are institutionalized, once again it is overwhelmingly probable that infants, whether male or female, learn about such relationships initially from their mothers, despite the fact that their relationships with their mothers at the time they learn about such relationships are never predominantly avoidant. This might, in turn (quite apart from how much of Freud one is prepared to accept), imply that the original embodiment of "the outsider" for both males and females is an adult male—ordinarily the father, or perhaps the mother's brother in matrilineal contexts. One of the matters that students of religion have never satisfactorily explained is how male embodiments of the deity were ever conceived. Perhaps sacredness always involves some element of avoidance and hence smacks more of males than females. Female embodiments of deities are also usually formidable for the faithful.

If the presence of some predominantly intimate relationships is universal for human beings, and if it is possible, probable, or in fact true that there are peoples or other mammals who are not characterized by predominantly avoidant relationships, then the emergence of such relationships is almost certainly a matter of social evolution. If a history of conquest by "outsiders" is involved, it is not difficult to see how avoidant relationships could evolve or be instituted. But predominantly avoidant relationships have probably characterized even those who have not been in contact with other peoples. *If this is so, predominantly avoidant relationships almost certainly have developed out of interfamily interdependencies.*

Although many instances of predominantly avoidant family relationships may be cited, those could conceivably have been derivative of relationships that made up early, primitive forms of government—that is, primitive forms of dispute-resolution arising from the interdependencies of two or more families. One would expect such relationships to be especially characteristic of the relationships a family head (or some counterpart of that person) has with other family members.

Fathers may have relatively restricted relationships with their infants and young children, but it is difficult to see how they can have predominantly avoidant relationships with them, if they have any at all. It would seem highly likely, after all, that predominantly avoidant relationships have to be learned by children after they have learned about predominantly intimate ones. *Predominantly intimate relationships are basic to human beings; predominantly avoidant ones are specialized.*

Perhaps one can observe similar phenomena in prides of lions and herds of horses. It may hold true for several of the primate species, but, alas, there are no elegant, puristically biological reductions of any of these possibilities. If one assumes that evolution is also relevant for human beings in the social sense, the following question immediately presents itself: What, if any, is the survival value of predominantly avoidant relationships? *This assumes for the moment that such relationships are not irrelevant or in the process of being selected against.* They certainly show no signs of the latter, unless one can mount an argument that the presence of predominantly avoidant relationships somehow threatens everyone today. But such an argument smacks more of ideology than of any attempt at scientific analysis.

5. Goal-Orientation Aspects

The polar distinction for goal-orientation aspects of relationships is that between individualistic and responsible. The criteria for individualistic goal orientation have nothing to do with selfishness, but rather with whether each actor concerned is, ideally speaking, expected to be the sole referent determinant of her or his behavior in the context of the relationship. The individual decides where his or her interests lie without regard for whether the other parties to the relationship achieve their goals. Ideally speaking, members of predominantly responsible relationships, in seeking their own goals, must take into consideration whether the goals of the other members of the relationship are being or will be realized. Both considerations always take place in a framework of what Durkheim saw as the noncontractual elements of contract. The modern-day relationship between a businessperson and a customer, as ordinarily perceived, is predominantly individualistic. That is to say, within certain canons of honesty and the like (i.e., noncontractual elements), the businessperson is not responsible for making sure that the customer really gets what she or he wants, let alone whether the customer really wants it or should want it. At the other pole, the parent-child relationship (for all known societies whose members are operating in a reasonably stable fashion) is institutionalized as predominantly responsible.[13] Ideally speaking, the parent is supposed to be concerned with the goals of the child while achieving her or his own goals, even if the only goal is to honor the ancestors. The parent-child relationship is, of course, highly asymmetrical because, for a good part of the relationship, the child may not comprehend what the parent's goals are or even have a clear idea of her or his own. That is certainly true in infancy and early childhood.

Here again, as in everything else, the earliest context of such relationships and the critical one for nearly all people at all times in their early stages of existence, if not throughout their lifetimes, has been and remains the family. *Family relationships are always institutionalized as predominantly responsible, although particular ones may be institutionalized as predominantly avoidant.* As indicated above, they may be highly asymmetrical, but when questions about goal orientations can be meaningfully asked of all parties to the relationship, the relationship is institutional-

---

13. Of course, some societies do go out of existence. Such descriptive material as we have on the IK illustrates this. IK parents seem to have dramatically reduced their levels of responsible treatment of their offspring and vice versa. See Turnbull (1972).

ized as predominantly responsible from the point of view of all parties. Parents are expected to be concerned with their children's welfare, and their children in some respects are always expected to honor their parents. This holds true of all of the family relationships.

In predominantly individualistic relationships, the various parties to a relationship may, within certain canons of honesty and the like, treat one another purely instrumentally. The parties to a predominantly responsible relationship never may. One obviously must keep in mind that ideal, not actual, patterns are being discussed here. Actually speaking, some of the parties to a predominantly individualistic relationship may treat others involved as ends in themselves—they may be actually quite responsible in these respects. Correspondingly, the parties to predominantly responsible relationships may in fact treat others involved instrumentally. When children treat their parents this way, their conduct is generally described as "unfilial" or "thoughtless" or by whatever similar term exists in their vocabulary. The Tagalog epithet for such conduct in the Philippines, for example, is *walang hiya* ("without shame"). It is the worst, most insulting thing one can call a Filipino. Probably no languages are devoid of such terms.

The people who rear infants and handle young children are not only expected to treat them in a predominantly responsible fashion but also to do so in some family context. All human beings are thus habituated to predominantly responsible relationships. Again, of course, they learn about such things initially from their mothers. As indicated throughout this study in so many other connections, human beings have to learn about predominantly individualistic relationships, if they learn about them at all, from a base of habituation to predominantly responsible ones.

The predominantly responsible relationship, ideally speaking, is a basic pattern for all human beings. All human beings have experienced some predominantly responsible relationships, but many, perhaps, have never experienced any predominantly individualistic ones, ideally or even actually speaking. For most societies, the overwhelming majority of all relationships are, ideally speaking, predominantly responsible.

The enormous proliferation of predominantly individualistic relationships, which are so much taken for granted in highly modernized settings, is a bizarre development in human history. This was not the case for all of those in human history who lived out the vast majority of their lives within eyeshot and/or earshot of some other members of their own family—that is, for most people before modernization. On the whole, predominantly individualistic relationships were exceedingly rare, if they existed at all, and, ideally speaking, were overwhelmingly likely to characterize relations with outsiders or strangers, when and if such relationships existed. The ready acceptance of predominantly individualistic relationships, which characterizes relatively modernized societies, never existed for most people.

Even in relatively modernized contexts, predominantly individualistic relationships are found in a general context of predominantly responsible ones. *Predominantly responsible relationships are basic for any society. Predominantly individualistic relationships are specialized, and are almost invariably specialized within any particular social context.* No society can therefore be accurately described as individualistic or even, more properly, as predominantly individualistic.[14] To do so, once again, is to commit the fallacy of misplaced dichotomies.

14. Although it would be out of place to speculate at length on this matter here, it may at least be suggested that the kind of emphasis on predominantly individualistic relationships that many of the members of relatively modernized societies take for granted may well turn out to have been something of a historical sport. These relationships were

Even in situations where predominantly individualistic relationships are not institutionalized, they may nonetheless crop up in actual cases. The most likely actual case is what may be termed *individualism by default°*. Under many circumstances, actors are forced to fall back on their own resources for decision making. The isolated stranger is perhaps the most extreme case of this sort. Individualism by default may also be forced on one by virtue of the fact that parents, siblings, kin, and troops of friends may not be available.

Given that a predominantly individualistic relationship has been institutionalized, the longer it persists, the greater is the probability that predominantly responsible elements will creep in, actually if not ideally. It is difficult for all parties to a relationship to maintain a predominantly instrumental relationship with one another when the relationship persists over a long period of time. The concept of honor among thieves illustrates a "responsible" element. The obverse does not hold.

6. Stratification Aspects

Stratification is here distinguished between predominantly hierarchical and nonhierarchical relationships. Again, these are polar terms, although egalitarian relationships may constitute a special subcategory of the latter. Egalitarian relationships possess explicit expectations that the parties to the relationship be treated without any reference to differences in power and responsibility. Non-

---

certainly critical in the development of relatively modernized societies, but they may be phased out in the evolution of modernized societies themselves. As social situations become more and more highly interdependent, predominantly individualistic relationships, while offering many degrees of freedom, as in the case of market phenomena, also carry with them far-reaching possibilities for the spread of effects which the members of the system may choose to decry and abandon.

hierarchical relationships, as a general category, may include ones that are nonhierarchical only by virtue of the fact that the question of hierarchy simply never gets raised. The vast majority of fleeting, casual contacts with strangers, which moderns take so much for granted, are nonhierarchical in this general sense. For our present purposes, a relationship will be considered more or less hierarchical if the members are expected to be ranked differently and if actions in the relationship are differentiated according to these rankings.

Nearly all social relationships have been, are, and will be predominantly hierarchical. There is absolutely no reason to think that *ur relationships*° were either egalitarian or predominantly nonhierarchical, despite all romantic political thought, from Rousseau on up or down, about primitive peoples or humans in general. Most modern peoples have been habituated to pay lip service to egalitarianism, but one has only to look around to see that few relationships are institutionalized as nonhierarchical or egalitarian, either ideally or actually. In modern contexts egalitarianism is often a utopian pattern with varying implications.

All known family patterns are predominantly hierarchical. Hierarchy within family contexts is overwhelmingly likely to be based on absolute- and relative-age distinctions, and distinctions regarding generation and sex. Beyond that common core of distinctions, families may vary a great deal. But how they vary is based on hierarchical distinctions the members choose to make, not on the institutionalization of egalitarian or nonhierarchical distinctions. Many of the relationships described as predominantly egalitarian are institutionalized as such only in terms of an actor's access to them, and even these are not ordinarily institutionalized as predominantly egalitarian or nonhierarchical once access to them has been determined. Equal access is no guarantee or predictor of egalitarian behavior.

Despite all talk about human interest in "freedom" and individual distaste for hierarchy, it should be obvious that few individuals have ever believed that "she or he governs best who governs least," but, rather, that "she or he governs best who governs most locally." Furthermore, a good case can be made that there appears to be only one relationship that is universally present in all known societies and that is generally institutionalized as predominantly egalitarian. That relationship is friendship, as discussed earlier (see pp. 58, 64, and 93). The concept of friendship involves the idea that all the parties to the relationship have identical rights and obligations. Such relationships may be quite important both to the individuals concerned and, in terms of their integration, to their society. Nothing of ongoing importance to the peoples concerned, however, has ever been based primarily on friendship relations: not the rearing of children, not the formation of marriages, not the governance of human beings, not the basic gathering of sustenance, not the maintenance of rituals, not even the creation of songs. One reason is simple: Any egalitarian relationship is vulnerable to being fractured at any moment at the whim of any party to the relationship. Anything based on egalitarianism is highly unstable—even problematic.

There is yet another matter to be considered. *Any given relationship initially institutionalized as predominantly nonhierarchical or egalitarian that persists long is increasingly likely to become hierarchical in actuality, if it has not been so from the very beginning.* A given friendship is not institutionalized as predominantly hierarchical, but most friendships have a dominant member as surely as do packs of wolves. The "Alpha" friend is usually quite easy to distinguish.

Hierarchical relationships are basic to all human beings; nonhierarchical ones are specialized, if they exist at all. For the overwhelming majority of all people, nonhierarchical or egalitarian relationships have never constituted any considerable portion of all their relationships. Even in the most highly modernized contexts, all relatively non-hierarchical relationships are embedded in a general setting of hierarchical ones. As indicated above, family relationships are predominantly hierarchical. The ability to distinguish or maintain predominantly nonhierarchical relationships is always developed from a base of habituation to hierarchical ones. Insofar as any nonhierarchical relationship can be said to characterize any other mammalian species, they too were developed on a grounding of overwhelming habituation to hierarchical relationships.

In relatively modernized settings, fleeting, casual contacts with strangers have become profuse and are institutionalized as predominantly nonhierarchical. But if such contacts are prolonged for whatever reasons, they change toward hierarchy.

One should expect—indeed, it is advanced as a generalization here—that all human beings learn initially about hierarchies in a family context from their mothers. Insofar as they learn nonhierarchical relationships, including egalitarian ones, during infancy and early childhood, they learn those from their mothers. There probably always is some learning about nonhierarchical possibilities from mothers, if only in a residual sense. But these may be only lightly stressed, if stressed at all. Hierarchical emphases show no general tendency to break down in the direction of nonhierarchical emphases.

SOME GENERAL FEATURES

Relationship aspects tend to cluster, as I suggest elsewhere (Levy 1970, esp. pp. 169–72, 810). The most generally encountered aspects in a relationship are those that are predominantly arational, particularistic, functionally diffuse, intimate, responsible, and hierarchical. In notational terms, such a relationship can be described as y_1,

y_2, y_3, y_4, y_5, and x_6. It can be maintained that whenever a relationship is institutionalized as predominantly rational, universalistic, and functionally specific (x_1, x_2, or x_3), it will also be predominantly avoidant (x_4) and hierarchical (x_6) as well. A relationship that is predominantly arational, particularistic, and functionally diffuse (y_1, y_2, or y_3) may be either predominantly avoidant (x_4) or intimate (y_4), but it will also be predominantly responsible and, most probably, hierarchical (y_5 and x_6) as well.

Given a relationship that is institutionalized as predominantly rational, universalistic, functionally specific, avoidant, individualistic, and hierarchical (x_1, x_2, x_3, x_4, x_5, and x_6), the longer it persists, the more likely it will take on predominantly arational, particularistic, functionally diffuse, intimate, and responsible features (y_1, y_2, y_3, y_4, and y_5). The predominantly arational, particularistic, functionally diffuse, intimate, responsible, and hierarchical aspects (y_1, y_2, y_3, y_4, y_5, and x_6) are not correspondingly vulnerable. The most stable form of all the relationship aspects is the predominantly hierarchical relationship, which never tends to become predominantly egalitarian or nonhierarchical. Except for y_6 (nonhierarchical), "y" aspects are apparently both more stable and are more easily accommodated by human beings than are x_1, x_2, x_3, x_4, and x_5 aspects (i.e., rational, universalistic, functionally specific, avoidant, and individualistic aspects)— whether in modern contexts or not.

It would seem clear that everyone initially learns about relationship aspects in a family context as one in some sense initially learns about practically everything that underlies subsequent learning. Certainly, learning about nonfamily relationships, and habituation to them, takes place in a family context and is usually taught by mothers. Just as sex-role differentiation is the first learned form of human variance and as the family is the basis for all "we-they" distinctions, *all relationships, as they have evolved in human contexts, must be either extensions of family relationships or specific differentiations from them.* The common extension of family governance into clan or lineage governance, where those exist, is universal. Those extensions, in turn, must have generated the original organizational context to which some such term as "government" may be applied. In their initial development, about which one can do little but speculate, governmental organizations must have been intimately bound up with family and other kin organizations. The same would be true of neighborhood organizations, village organizations, and the like. *The family specifically, kinship in general, and neighborhood organizations must have been the building blocks for all subsequent human organizational development.* Even in modern settings, wherein they seem to lose their striking predominance, these family-styled organizations still underlie all the rest. And *the original teacher, the basic teacher, is always and everywhere the mother.*

11

Fathers

This entire work is on touchy subjects, but the touchiest subject of all may well be *fathers*. What is stated here is not about what some fathers do in some societies at some times, but only about what all fathers do or do not do insofar as a case can be made for that. Of interest here is whether what follows is, at least for the moment, tenable and clear cut. Given the variations of time and place and of individual fathers, there may well be, or have been, individual fathers for whom these generalizations may not hold. Nevertheless, the hypothesis here is that these generalizations will hold for the overwhelming majority of fathers now and in the past. Current preferences for change in these respects have not yet become generalized among the members of any society. Again, no judgment of good, bad, or indifferent is intended, and nothing said here should in any way be taken as invidious. My focus in this chapter is on what was, what is, and even on what will be. I have no intention whatsoever of maintaining that whatever was, or is, is "right" or "wrong," or that it might be "right" or "wrong" for the future. This asymmetry of parental attention is discussed primarily as a fact of the past and the present—whatever its future may be.

Axiom V (see p. 20) asserts a highly asymmetrical relationship in the ratio of female to male supervision, direct handling, control, and care of the infant and young child. This is thought to be highly invariant from one society to another. Whether the asymmetry is of the ratio 19 to 1 as opposed to 15 to 1 may vary, but it never approaches 1 to 1 or 1 to 15. Axiom VI (see p. 21) holds, however, that regardless of the father's role in infant and childhood learning, he is likely to be present in some family context a substantial part of most days—even in the most modernized contexts. This axiom rests on the fact that until quite recently in history the vast majority of all human beings, say more than 85 percent, spent the vast majority of all of their waking and sleeping hours, say 85 percent, within eyeshot and/or earshot of some other member(s) of their own families. It by no means follows that the father would be within eyeshot or earshot of his infants or young children for any such proportion of his time. The other family member(s) could be an older son, a brother, a father, or a nephew.

Societies also vary, without affecting this alleged factor, in how much time fathers spend away from home, even when they are accompanied by a family member. This is particularly likely in societies whose menfolk go on deep-sea fishing expeditions, trading excursions, hunting forays, and so forth. Nevertheless, a considerable part of a father's time is probably spent in the family context in which the mother and infant or young child are also present.

Three points apply here: They have to do with the probability of a father's presence, the asymmetry of paternal care, and the variability of what a father does when he is in contact with his offspring. First, the probability of a father being in close proximity to an infant or very young child varies widely, whereas, by contrast at least, the probability of a mother being in such proximity does not—she is likely to be present all or the vast majority of the time. Second, *what* the father does when he is present varies greatly. Even when he is present, the maternal assymetry in direct supervisory care and handling of the infant is likely to be great. He may play with but not feed or clean the infant, and so forth. The mother is still the caretaker and caregiver of first and last resort. Third, the father varies greatly in how much of what he does he actually does. The mother varies relatively little in how often she is present, in what she does, or in how much of what she does she actually does.

One of the best articles on this score has been written by M. W. West and M. J. Konner (1976). Among other things, they relate father-infant proximity to subsistence adaptation and family organization. They find father-infant relationships are relatively close among gatherers "who represent the sociocultural form that existed for 99% of human history" (p. 212). Although this may be correct, gatherers of this sort hardly come anywhere close to constituting a substantial majority of all human beings who have ever lived, and they are almost certainly a small minority of all such human beings.[1] Nevertheless, West and Konner's scholarship represents a kind of careful effort, which, if carried further, will have enormous implications for this entire subject. Findings along these lines may someday contradict Axiom V. If anything, they seem to reinforce Axiom VI (pp. 21–22).

As suggested in chapter 2, hypotheses 16 and 17, two generalizations can be made about the relevance of fathers in these respects:

16. Infants initially learn about males in general and fathers in particular via their mothers' subjective view of what fathers are like.

---

1. The approximately half a million years of the existence of such people certainly does contain the major opportunity for genetic mutations and adjustment of *Homo sapiens*. That period has presumably covered a hundred times as many generations as the past five thousand years. Even for a slow-maturing species, that is a considerable difference. In any case, that period does not appear to have produced any built-in mechanisms that contradict or make unlikely the human traits dealt with here.

17. Because a father is likely to be present and observed in a family context a good part of many days, an infant's subjective view of a father is likely to be an amalgam of a mother's subjective view and that infant's observation of and interaction with a father.

The first of these two must almost certainly follow from the axioms presented. For hypothesis 16 to be false, the mother would have to communicate little or nothing about males to the individual infant or young child—an unlikely scenario. All young children of all societies, regardless of how much their fathers are present, have developed concepts of what males, as opposed to females, are like, of whether they themselves are males or females, and of what are appropriate behaviors for males and females. Furthermore, while the presence of a male and the contexts in which one is present may vary considerably, the presence of a female, at least in the form of a mother, does not. She is present practically all the time for infants and young children and for a sizable proportion of time for most of the older children as well. This nearly constant presence of the mother is subject to variation as the mobility of a child increases, but it probably varies little for young children of either sex. If it does, it varies primarily for male children (see pp. 182–84). Before this variation of the mother's presence takes place (if it does take place in the case of males), the male child has already learned a great deal about male roles, as distinguished from female roles, from his mother and, presumably, has also been taught by her to identify himself as a male.

Given the asymmetry of care, supervision, and so forth, in addition to the improbability of mothers having no subjective views of what fathers or males in general are like, or of not communicating any views if they do have them, hypothesis 16 (p. 22) either holds or must give way to more puristically biological explanations.

Hypothesis 17, however, raises an entirely new range of questions. In all of the preceding discussion, little has been said about the subjectivity, observation, and interaction of the infant or young child. Attention has rested on the sort of individual most likely to teach, influence, and care for an infant. But the child's subjective states are the essence of understanding how infants and young children learn and develop.

The asymmetry of parental attention is so great, however, that whether an infant or a child is a genius or an idiot, female or male, sensitive or insensitive, a fast learner or a slow learner, the individual learns and is overwhelmingly inculcated via his or her mother. Not the least of what a mother inculcates on a child is her subjective view of what mothers and other women generally are like. While all that is being done, that mother is there, presumably being observed by and interacting with the infant or child. In that sense, the relationship is direct.

The infant's (or child's) relationship with the father, however, has an inherent indirectness. In the first place, the presence of the father is highly variable. But whether the father is present or not, the infant (or child) will learn about him from the mother. However much her subjective view may coincide with what is objectively correct, a subjective view is nonetheless being conveyed. The infant cannot observe or interact with a subjective view; the father must be present for any observation or interaction to take place. *On occasion, such observation and interaction may coincide with the mother's inculcations about males on the infant or child, but it is not mainly so as it is in the case of the mother.*

What a mother is, or says she is, and the infant's observation and interaction with her are, as stated before, simultaneous. This is not necessarily the case in the infant's observation and interaction with a father, and it almost certainly is not the case for a large proportion of the infant's learning about males in general and fathers in particular. For an infant, a mother must be what she is. What a mother says about herself, or some similar person, is part of what she is. What she says about the father or males in general is also part of what she is. What she inculcates on the infant, male or female, about a father or other males, however, in some sense separates the objective and the subjective.

How infants and children learn about their fathers is probably the first, or one of the first, learned forms of comparing what one is told or otherwise taught with what one observes directly. If the father were never present, of course, an infant or child would be left with nothing but the mother's view of him. Until interaction with quite a different set of actors takes place, an infant would have no opportunity to compare his or her observations with a mother's subjective version of the father and other males.

In one form or another, that has never been the case for infants and children of any known society. They always have some opportunity to observe a father or some other male(s). There is always this opportunity—this inescapable opportunity—to compare what one has been "told" or "shown" with what one observes about fathers or whatever. This opportunity to compare exists and inheres in the infant's situation despite the fact that what one has been told or shown may, and almost certainly does, importantly condition what one observes and how one interacts with that.

The search for universals with which to challenge sociobiologists or to titillate one's own curiosity about fathers and their influence on infants and young children is frustrating in the extreme for two reasons. First, the influence of fathers is so marginal, given the asymmetry alleged in Axiom V, and so derivative of mothers' teaching, even if direct paternal influence is not marginal, that it is hard to know what to say. Second, societies vary so

enormously in how and in what respects fathers are marginal and what mothers think of them. A good part of
the time fathers may not be present at all. How much and
what they do when they are present are subject to much
more variation than what mothers do, especially relative
to infants. Whether mothers are Lapps, Lithuanians,
Greeks, or Jews, Asians, blacks, whites, or greens, they
all feed infants, they all handle them, they all teach them
to speak, they all do all of the things mentioned throughout this book. At least that is the hypothesis presented
here. *Mothers vary more in how they do all these things than
in what they do; fathers vary both in the things they do and
how they do them.* Even when fathers are present, the old
American song admits, "Everybody works but father. He
sits around all day!" which also seems to hold with regard
to infant and child care—with suitable allowance for folk
exaggeration, of course. But the song doesn't exaggerate
so much, by contrast with the roles of mothers.

The direct impact of males on the development of infants and young children is highly variable and recalci-
trant to generalization. Males always have some impact,
however, on the females with whom they live, and vice
versa. Despite the variability in when, how much, and
what fathers do for offspring, one can generalize about
any society as follows: *The major impact males have on the
development of infants and young children is a function of the
impact those males have on the females who mother.*

The picture changes after the age of three, four, or
five, but even that tends to defy generalization. Until relatively modernized societies developed sometime in the
nineteenth century, the overwhelming majority of all
peoples, in fact probably all of them without exception,
practiced sexually segregated education for adulthood.
This education did not involve schools, of which there
were few, if any. In general, however, the young boys
went off to the fields or fishnets or wherever they went

with their fathers or older brothers, and the young girls continued with their mothers or older sisters. This segregation of supervision held even when the girls and their mothers also went off to the fields and fishnets as well.

That changed, however, with the development of relatively modernized societies, where the fathers and older brothers, if there are any, cannot take the younger boys to work with them. Young children go to school now. In many, if not most, of those school systems education, particularly in the earlier grades, tends to be conducted by females and is coeducational. *Under these modernized conditions, the role of women in the development of offspring becomes even greater.* It remains largely as it was from birth to the age of three, four, or five. From the age of three, four, or five onward a mother or mother surrogate continues to be the person on whom the direct care and handling of the offspring depends. When male offspring are off "in school," the person who serves as a mother surrogate is the teacher, who is also very likely to be female. Moreover, the children are increasingly unlikely to be handled on a sexually segregated basis. With rare exceptions, modern school systems are coeducational.

Under these dispensations the males of modernized contexts have changed more radically from the males of other social contexts than have their sisters. They now continue largely under the direct care and supervision of older females from birth to young adulthood rather than from birth through early childhood. The relevance of both hypotheses 16 and 17 under modernized conditions tends to be extended virtually right up to young adulthood. This extension is qualified, of course, by the influence of their same-sex peers.

One is tempted to say that it is difficult to understand why males so generally, especially under modern conditions, think other males are such an important, formative influence in their lives. There must be a great deal more to this perception than any of the generalizations presented here would give one any reason to think or believe. What does not seem problematic is that a considerable amount of this perception on the part of both males and females is formed after early childhood, *if* male influence is in fact the independent variable. Even so, it is inculcated on a foundation that must in some sense be preparatory for this perception, and that is inculcated on infants and children largely by their mothers. I doubt that male influence is the independent variable most people seem to assume.

Prior to modernization all infants were initially socialized by their mothers. The males were then taught their adult occupational roles by their fathers after early childhood. The females continued under their mothers' supervision and were also taught their adult occupational roles by their mothers, as they had earlier been taught virtually all else. Under modernized conditions fathers have become, in a sense, even more marginal, although their role in the care and supervision of infants and very young children may be increasing. Whatever tendencies exist in that direction, none of them has yet shown any substantial probability of either reducing maternal asymmetry to a more nearly egalitarian distribution or reversing the asymmetry of parental influence. *If they do not change, insofar as the offspring of either sex come to think their fathers or other males more important as influences on their lives than their mothers, they will continue to learn to do so from their mothers—at least initially. And they will continue to be wrong in thinking so.*

My mama done tol' me
When I was in knee-pants. . . .

From "Blues in the Night"

Glossary

This glossary, with adaptations and additions, borrows copiously from the author's earlier books, especially *The Structure of Society* (1952), *Some Aspects of the Analysis of Family Structure* (with Coale et al. 1965), and *Modernization and the Structure of Societies* (1966).

absolute age   A basis of role differentiation. Absolute age is used as a criterion for assigning a particular type of role, and individuals are deemed eligible for such roles by belonging to a particular age span. That span is conceived as being such that an individual can belong to one, and only one, such span at any one time. Thus, one may be identified as an infant who acts like a child or as a child who acts like an infant. One cannot, however, be both an infant and a child at the same time. Four absolute-age distinctions are always made in one form or another. These are infancy, childhood, adulthood, and old age. Most societies are characterized by more than these four categories, but the various categories distinguished always cut across these four and exhaust them in one form or another. See *age*.

absolutism	A pattern of political allocation for which most or all power is invested in a ruler and her or his representatives. Absolutism particularly involves the ability and willingness to suppress dissent and to obtain conformity by coercion if necessary.
achievement	See *universalistic*.
actual (structures or patterns)	Refers to the patterns (structures) that are observed regardless of the professed, or ideal, patterns. Thus, for example, one may say that, *ideally,* the members of U.S. society consider bullying a bad thing, but many of them *actually* engage in bullying. See *ideal (ideal patterns or structures)*.
adaptationism	See *functional teleology*.
adulthood	That period in life during which the average member of a society is held to be capable of full responsibility for her or his activity.
aesthetic	Of or pertaining to considerations of beauty.
affect (affective)	Indications of pleasurable or painful significance to the actor, and of approval or disapproval of the object or state that occasions the reaction, and those reactions to stimuli that are commonly catalogued under the term "emotions"—i.e., anger, hate, fear, love, pity, etc.
affinal	Related by marriage; e.g., a brother-in-law.
age	The period of time during which something (including someone) may be said to have existed. Thus, one may speak of the age of an individual or the age of an institution, or of an organization, or of a building, etc.

allocative puberty   The mistaken notion that allocation, whether of goods and services, power and responsibility, or whatever, is of negligible relevance for individuals until they near or reach adulthood. This concept is used to poke fun at the idea that allocation for humans, like sexual maturation, occurs only as a preparation for adulthood in the near approach to adulthood, or as the sign or rite of passage denoting adulthood.

anabolism   Constructive metabolism, as opposed to catabolism.

analytic structure (or aspect or distinction)   Patterned aspects of action or other phenomena that are not even theoretically capable of concrete separation from other patterns of action or phenomena. Thus, the distinction between the mass, shape, and color of a chair or the economic, political, and solidarity aspects of a society are distinctions of analytic structures. Distinctions among the arms, legs, and back of a chair, or the families, the villages, and merchant firms of a society are distinctions of concrete structures. See *concrete structure*.

apathy   The cessation of individual motivation, conceived of here as capable of variation by degrees. Thus, one may speak of a more or less apathetic individual or set of individuals.

arational (arationality)   All nonrational action that is not irrational.

ascribed (ascription)   See *particularism*.

avoidant   Relationships characterized by minimal, formal contact, and the restraint or overt affective displays.

basic   Any quality or characteristic that is common, or expected to be common, to all of the members of any set. Thus, for example, family systems of some sort are basic to any society; the use of language is basic to all human beings capable of learning a language.

basic   That cognition that all the members of
cognition   any set under discussion are assumed to share. See *cognition*.

biological   Having to do with any living physical phenomena.

biological descent   Derivation of living physical phenomena from other, older living physical phenomena.

capricious   Any particularism that invokes nonger-
particularism   mane (or irrelevant) criteria, although the criteria may involve no social barring, e.g., to insist that only red-headed individuals be hired to operate lathes. The criterion of red-headedness could be germane for some relationships, for example those involving certain forms of genetic analysis. See *particularism*.

catabolism   Destructive metabolism, as opposed to anabolism.

cathectic (cathexis)   See *affect*.

centralization   The organization of the action of the members of a social system about one or more foci. Complete centralization of a society would consist of having a single member make and carry out all decisions and determine all coordination; any departure from this constitutes some element of decentralization. Rule by members of a committee is not so centralized as rule by a single individual, etc. Complete centralization and complete authoritarianism would be identical. Neither is possible.

certainty situations Situations in which unanticipated factors are not relevant or in which the actors do not anticipate unknown factors. Situations may be certainty situations objectively and/or subjectively.

change A unit or aspect of a phenomenon will have undergone change if the state of any elements of the model used to analyze the unit varies from one point in time to another. Change will vary according to the level of generality of one's model. If one is considering simply the presence of a family system in any society, the only form of change is from the presence to the absence of a family system for that society. If one is considering the type of descent system characteristic of the family systems of a given society, variation of the descent system from a patrilineal to a matrilineal one will constitute a change.

charisma The quality of being able to determine for one's followers the obligations for which they are responsible and the goals toward which they should strive as the referents of action. A charismatic leader may be defined as an individual who, as far as his followers are concerned, can transfer transcendental referents of action to empirical ones.

child See *childhood*.

childhood That absolute-age distinction made in all known societies covering the period between infancy and adulthood. In some, but not all, societies this period may be broken down into subcategories, one of which is frequently distinguished as adolescence, which may be conceived of as specifically interstitial to childhood and adulthood. Childhood is a period during which the individual, while no longer absolutely dependent on others for all factors necessary for survival, nevertheless depends on them for instruction and guidance in the institutionally permissible and necessary behaviors required of individual members of his or her society. Childhood, as a minimum, implies the ability to speak the language of the society (or the portion of it in terms of which the individual acts) and to walk.

class Any set of individuals with any designated set of common characteristics. Thus, all individuals six feet tall could be described in these terms as a class—so could all landowners. Ordinary usage of the term rockets between this definition and that which posits a membership unit of some sort. Frequently encountered usages such as "the bourgeois class" often rocket back and forth between these two definitions without any warning. On the whole, the concept of class has confusing social applications, though this need not be the case. The concept of class as a membership unit is quite another matter. Class as a membership unit is a system of action involving all of the representatives of a set who share among other characteristics the characteristic of being members of that unit. An individual may, however, be a representative of a class in the more general sense without being a "class member." One may, for example, be one of a set of all gravediggers without belonging to any gravediggers' organization. It is essential that one avoid confusion of a set of representatives of any class with a concept of class as a membership unit involving a set of class members.

class interests The goals, ends, etc., that can be said to characterize the representatives or members of a particular class. Again, this concept in ordinary usage rockets between two meanings (see *class*).

class structure The patterns of actions that can be attributed to class identification.

closed class A set of individuals with common characteristics based at least in part on presumed or simulated biological descent. Recruitment of members for a closed class system always involves the family context of other representatives or members of the closed class.

coeducation The inculcation of knowledge about phenomena, ideas (including those with empirical and/or nonempirical referents), abstract concepts, and the social patterns of the referent systems in settings that involve both males and females as students.

cognition Knowledge or understanding of an empirical situation or phenomenon, of abstractions in general, and of nonempirical concepts and elements.

cognitive aspect Refers to how memory and analysis are involved in a relationship.

cohort A set of individuals who share the occurrence of an event such as birth, marriage, graduation, etc. Following Norman Ryder.

communication	The activity or process whereby one (or more individuals) of a given species infers from the behavior (whether language of oral and/or written types, gesture, or posture) of another individual (or group of individuals) of the same or different species an idea or feeling or state of affairs that the other individual(s) is trying to convey or conveys inadvertently.
concept	A name for the members of a given class of any sort. In science, concepts may be more or less precisely defined, must have empirical referents, and are more or less fruitful for the formation of hypotheses. In science, concepts are not valid or invalid.
conceptual scheme	Concepts that are used in conjunction with one another for any particular purpose.
concrete social system	See *concrete structure*.
concrete structure	Those patterns that characterize units involving a set of members in social action. Such a set is, at least in theory, capable of physical separation in time and/or space from the membership of other, similar units with, of course, the possibility of overlapping memberships. Societies, which are themselves concrete structures, involve sets of members (i.e., a plurality of interacting individuals involved in a system of action primarily oriented to the system concerned). See *expedient members* and *genuine members*.
conformity	The extent to which an individual's behavior in fact coincides with a normative expectation. See also *institution*.

conjugal (nuclear) family	See *family, conjugal.*
consanguine	Related by blood, i.e., by biological descent; e.g., son, grandchild, etc.
consumption	The utilization of goods and services.
consumption roles	Social positions differentiated on the basis of utilization of goods and/or services.
content	As a subcategory of solidarity, the type of relationship that is to exist and the members between (or among) whom it is to exist.
culturalization	The inculcation or development of culture. See *culture.*
culture	The system of action of a society considered apart from its involvement of a plurality of interacting individuals, i.e., apart from operation in terms of it. The concepts *culture* and *society* refer to different ways of looking at the same thing. The two are analytically, not concretely, distinct. The concept of society (or social) focuses attention on the patterns of the unit considered in operation. The concept of culture focuses attention on the patterns considered qua patterns. Defined in this way, it is always possible to keep culture distinct from society, though one cannot talk about either culture or society "causing" something about one or the other. One may, however, state generalizations such as: "Cultural feature x always changes in the direction of y," or "Because of an ineradicable interest in material betterment, modernized social patterns will always diffuse to nonmodernized contexts when contact is made," etc. N.B.: Neither culture nor society is

"more general," "better," "deeper," or "more significant" than the other—in scientific usage.

decentralization   The process of moving away from higher
(decentralized)   levels of coordination and control. Complete decentralization would require every individual to decide what to do and when to do it without reference to anyone else. There would be no accepted methods whereby one individual could coerce or influence another. Completely decentralized societies can no more exist than can completely centralized societies.

descent units   Those kinship units for which the membership and the nature of solidarity is determined, at least in part, by orientation to their biological relatedness to some ancestor.

distribution   The mode or manner in which elements of any sort are arranged, or come to be, in time and/or space or along other dimensions.

dysfunction   A condition, or state of affairs, that (1) results from operation (including mere persistence) in terms of a structure of a given unit through time and (2) lessens the adaptation or adjustment to the unit's setting, thus making for a lack of persistence (i.e., a change in, or dissolution) of the unit as defined of which the structure is a part or aspect. N.B.: Whether a given function is a eufunction (or a dysfunction) or not has no implications for good, bad, or indifference. For it to have implications of a normative sort, the criteria for considering the unit to be good, bad, or indifferent must be established, establishing thereby that its persistence is, in turn, good, bad, or indifferent.

early childhood

The period of childhood extending through the ages of three, four, or five years. See *childhood*.

economic allocation

The distribution of goods and services making up the income and output of the members of a concrete structure among the various members of the unit and among the members of that unit and of other units with which its members are in contact. N.B.: Acts of distribution are themselves economic allocations, in this case, of services.

economic self-sufficiency

A unit will be considered economically self-sufficient to the degree and in the respects that its membership acting in terms of its patterns (structures) can and does both produce and consume all of the goods and services necessary to and resulting from the operations in terms of the unit.

education

The inculcation of knowledge about phenomena, ideas (including those with empirical and/or nonempirical referents), abstract concepts, and the social patterns of the referent systems. Education can always be analyzed in terms of learning and teaching.

egalitarianism

See *egalitarian relationship*.

egalitarian relationship

One in terms of which all of the members treat one another without reference to any hierarchical considerations.

elegant biological reduction

Any phenomenon involving biological organisms, e.g., human beings, that can be demonstrated to be adequately explained for whatever purposes are at hand by the factors of species' heredity and the nonspecies' environment, in a highly generalized, parsimonious, scientific fashion.

An elegantly biologically reduced proposition ought to involve "something like" the role played by the development of the Periodic Tables of the Elements in the reduction of chemistry to a special case of physics.

elites   Individuals invidiously distinguished from others presumably on the basis of more or less highly prized characteristics, e.g., the "wealthy," the "highly educated," the "musically gifted," the "truly devout," the "highly skilled," the "sanctimonious," etc.

emotion   See *affect*.

empirical   Subject to sensory perception or to inference from sensory perception.

end   Any future state of affairs toward which action is oriented.

eufunction(al)   A condition or state of affairs that (1) results from operation (including mere persistence) in terms of a structure of a given unit through time and (2) increases or maintains adaptation or adjustment to the unit's setting, thus making for the persistence of the unit as defined, of which the structure concerned is a part or aspect. N.B.: Whether a given function is a eufunction (or a *dysfunction*°) or not has no implication for good, bad, or indifference. For it to have normative implications, the criteria for considering the unit to be good, bad, or indifferent must be established, establishing thereby that its persistence is, in turn, good, bad, or indifferent.

eufunctional   See *eufunction*.

expedient members	Those individuals who orient their action to the patterns of a particular concrete structure for instrumental purposes rather than because they find them "good" and/or acceptable as normative patterns. See *membership*.
expression	The type and limits of reaction, symbolic or otherwise, on the part of individuals or sets of individuals to the various phenomena with which they come in contact.
extended family	See *family, extended*.
external causes of change	Causes of change are external if they are dependent functions of (i.e., produced by) operation in terms of units other than the unit that is spoken of as changed.
faddism	The relatively rapid and intense alteration and application of means for relatively fixed ends. The rapid alteration of fashions in clothing, of some of the techniques of therapy in modern medical practice, of recreational forms, and the like, are all examples of this phenomenon.
fallacy of misplaced dichotomies	The use of a dichotomous (or binary or dyadic) distinction to refer to polar distinctions with the possibility of infinite variations (or very large, finite variations) between the poles; i.e., the use of a binary distinction to describe a nonbinary distinction.
family	A kinship unit (or organization) for which membership is always oriented, at least in part, to biological descent and sexual intercourse. See *kinship units*.
family, conjugal	A family ordinarily having as members only a husband and a wife (or father and mother) and nonadult children if present.

Husband and wife, before they bear children, orient their behavior at least in part to the expectation that children, and hence descent considerations, may ensue.

family, extended A family unit characterized by the fact that, ideally speaking, all of the siblings of a given sex, usually the males, have their *family of procreation* as a continuation of their *family of orientation*. Siblings of the other sex "marry out of" their family of orientation.

family, multilineal conjugal A conjugal family whose members emphasize both matrilineal and patrilineal descent more or less equally.

family, nuclear See *family, conjugal.*

family, stem A family unit characterized by the fact that for one sibling, perhaps most often the eldest male sibling, the family of procreation is a continuation of his or her family of orientation. All other siblings, if any, become members of other families of procreation.

family foreign relations Involvement of some family members in relationships with individuals who are not members of their own family, especially, of course, those having implications for the family or families concerned, apart from a family member's simply being involved.

family of orientation The family context in which an individual is reared, usually from birth to adulthood, although there may be family systems for which individuals have more than one family of orientation; for example, they may switch units sometime during childhood or at the beginning of childhood.

family of procreation	The family context in which an individual has, and to some extent rears, her or his children.
family units	See *family*.
father	A male parent. One may distinguish between a puristically biologically defined father—i.e., the individual source of the sperm that fertilizes an ovum—and a socially defined one, i.e., anyone defined as a male parent whether on the puristically biological grounds stated above or on others. Social and biological tend to coincide in the overwhelming majority of social contexts but probably not so often as do social and biological mothers. "It is a wise father. . . ." See *mother*.
father surrogate	One who performs the functions usually associated with a father. Father surrogates are usually male.
father-time	The time spent by fathers in direct care and interaction with their offspring. See *father*.
feral children	Individuals abandoned by humans in infancy and reared in the wild by mammals of other species.
formal	A given type of action will be termed formalized or formal to the degree that its structures (but not necessarily all the specific obligations covered) are precisely and minutely defined and/or institutionalized for the context of action in which it appears, regardless of the specific individuals involved. N.B.: There is consequently an element of universalism about all formal patterns.
formality	See *formal*.

free goods   Any goods accessible to any and all individuals at no cost, i.e., without regard to any productivity by or income accruing to anyone. "The moon belongs to everyone. The best things in life are free."

friendship   A relationship for which the rights and obligations of the various parties are, ideally speaking, equal, and the solidarity is, ideally speaking, completely voluntary.

function   A condition or state of affairs resultant from operation (including mere persistence) in terms of a structure through time. N.B.: Function and structure are unusual concepts (like production and consumption, anabolism and catabolism) in that what is a function from one point of view is a structure from another. See *structure*.

functionally diffuse   Describes relationships for which the substantive definition—i.e., the activities or considerations of rights and obligations or performances that are covered by the relationship—is more or less vaguely defined and delimited. In terms of such a relationship, the burden of proof for declining a request by one party to the relationship rests, institutionally, on the person(s) wishing to decline the request, who must cite another, overriding consideration. Following early Parsons.

functionally specific   Describes relationships for which the substantive definition—i.e., the activities or considerations of rights and obligations or performances that are covered by the relationship—is precisely defined and delimited. In terms of such a relationship, the burden of proof for establishing as legitimate any special claim in terms of the relationship rests, institutionally, on the person(s) making the special claim. Following early Parsons.

functional requisite A generalized condition necessary for the maintenance of the unit with which it is associated given the level of the generalization of the definition, and the most general setting, of such a unit. N.B.: To hold that a given function exists because it is a requisite of a particular system is to commit a form of the fallacy of functional teleology, in this case, functional requisite teleology. Also, establishing a function as a functional requisite tells one nothing normative—nothing of whether it is good, bad, or indifferent.

functional teleology The fallacy of holding that a given function exists because of its implications for a given purpose or goal or end state of affairs. Thus: Teleology in general is usually illustrated by some such statement as "legs developed to wear pants," or "noses to bear spectacles." Functional teleology in a social context is well illustrated by the statement that the family developed *to* socialize children. It is not teleological to maintain that the "family developed and children are socialized in terms of it." It is functional teleology to maintain that the profuse, corded coat of the Komondor dog developed *to* protect it from weather and predators. What some biologists today call "adaptionism" is a form of functional teleology.

fundamentalistic reaction Behavior of individuals who are dissatisfied with a current changed context and long for and seek a return to what are regarded as the "good old days." Some of these always try to turn the clock back, but they never can. "The moving finger writes. . . ."

games Sport of any kind; play, frolic, or fun; an amusement or diversion. (*Webster's New International Dictionary*. 2d ed.)

generalized affirmative Any application of the term "yes" or its equivalent that has meaning independent of the actor's understanding of the substantive content of the question being asked. There exists in effect for human beings no such thing as a generalized affirmative. There exists no referent, as it were, of the generalized affirmative. The generalized affirmative is of no utility in selection. For the affirmative voice to be used intelligently, one must understand substantively the question asked.

generalized negative Rejection whether via the use of some such term as "no," or by gesture of whatever thing or stimulus is being advanced. If an individual is in interaction with an environment—say, a parent—that keeps offering the individual different alternatives, it is possible, for example, for an infant to select by continuous rejection. If an infant is wet, he (she) need not be mollified when presented with the breast or covered with a blanket. By using the generalized negative, the infant will persist in being unmollified until he or she is changed. Prior to the storage of much substantive material in the memory, infants characteristically do select by learning to use the generalized negative more or less efficiently. What constitutes efficiency in this context will be most importantly determined for human infants by the attentiveness and perceptivity of an infant's mother or mother surrogate. The form of the generalized negative that is most likely to be singled out and reinforced is crying. Crying is the first learned form of expression of rejection. All infants learn to cry more or less efficiently.

generation   The position of an individual relative to other individuals in terms of the number of births of individuals involved in his/her direct biological line of descent from some (arbitrarily chosen) ancestor in that line.

genuine members   Those individuals who are involved in a concrete structure by virtue of the fact that their actions for the purposes in hand are in fact primarily oriented to the system concerned. See *membership*.

germane particularism   Reckoning of the eligibility for membership in any relationship on the basis of criteria that some individuals are socially barred from possessing, but which criteria are relevant to the purposes for which the person is selected. Thus, at any given point in time, all individuals save one are ineligible to succeed to the throne of England, but given the relevance of the symbolism of continuity and tradition implicit in the position, the kinship criteria of the royal house are relevant.

goal   Any future state of affairs toward which action is oriented. See *end*.

goal-orientation aspect   That aspect of a relationship structure that focuses attention on what might be called "motivation." Here, one reckons the goals as determined on a more or less individualistic or a more or less responsible basis. See *individualistic* and *responsible*.

governance Having to do with the allocation of power and responsibility.

government A predominantly politically oriented organization that the members of a society regard as the most general, legitimate source of settlement of disagreements among members of two or more subsystems of that society. N.B.: The government of a society is not necessarily the "most powerful" subsystem of the society. Members of other subsystems may be able to marshal greater power than can the members of their government.

hierarchical The differential ranking of individuals, especially in terms of allocations of power and responsibility.

high modernization See *modernization, high*.

household A concrete unit whose members are always associated with some family unit. Households may involve, in addition to family member , family servants, various kin, friends, etc.

ideal (ideal patterns or structures) Any structures (or patterns) of behavior held to be "good" by an actor (or actors), usually institutionalized to some degree. For example, for a vast majority of the members of U.S. society, universal literacy is an ideal pattern. Hence it may be spoken of as an ideal pattern of U.S. society. See *institution*.

income The amount of money, goods, or services received over a given period of time by an individual or set of individuals.

individualism	A doctrine holding that any given actor is and/or should be the major, or sole, referent of decisions affecting his future or that of others with whom he or she interacts, regardless of whether those decisions are "altruistic" or "selfish." See also *individualistic*.
individualism by default	Exists when the fact that a given individual makes decisions affecting his or her future or the future of others with whom she or he interacts may be taken to be a function of the fact that alternative socially expected or institutionalized criteria or judgments are either unavailable, nonexistent, or irrelevant. See *individualism*.
individualistic	A given relationship is more or less individualistic to the degree that each of the parties to the relationship may be expected to calculate how best to secure maximum advantage from the relationship for himself or herself without regard to the goals (ends) sought by other parties to the relationship.
infancy (infants)	That period in the life cycle during which the ("average" or "normal") individual is completely dependent on the intervention of more fully developed individuals for survival. Individuals in this category (i.e., infants) are not able to walk, talk, or eat unaided. Acquisition of the ability to do these things marks the beginning of childhood.
informal	A given type of action will be termed informalized or informal to the extent that variations in its structure (or patterns) actually develop and/or are institutionalized

on the basis of the specific individuals involved at a specific time. There is, thus,
usually an element of particularism involved in informality.

informality   See *informal*.

institution   Normative pattern(s), conformity with
which is generally to be expected, and
failure to conform with which is met with
the moral indignation of and/or sanctions
by those individuals who are involved in
the same general social system and who
are aware of the failure (following early
Parsons circa 1937). One may distinguish
between the conformity aspect and the
sanctions aspect of any institution.

integrated theory   One which, in its derivation, is at least in
part deduced from other theories and/or
is logically interdependent with other theories.

integration   Eufunctional adaptation to a concrete
structure.

intensity   The state and degree of affect involved in
a relationship.

interfamily   Existing between or among members of
two or more families. See *family*.

intermediate ends   Future states of affairs toward which action may be (is) oriented and that are them-
selves means to further ends.

intimacy   A quality that places emphasis on direct
contact, "informality," and overt display
of affects.

intimate   See *intimacy*.

intrafamily   Common to internal family structure involving no nonfamily interdependencies. See *family*.

irrational   Action for which the objective and subjective ends of actions are both empirical but not identical. I.e., the actor(s) concerned will not reach the ends sought by the means employed. Their choice of means may be either a function of ignorance or error or some combination of the two.

isolated theory   One which in its derivation is not dependent in any way on other theories, or if it is, such derivation is not available or made apparent.

kinship structure   That portion of the total structure of a society for which, in addition to other orientations (sometimes equally, if not more, important), membership and the nature of the solidarity are to some extent, at least, determined by orientation to the facts of biological relatedness (descent) and/or sexual intercourse. N.B.: One may, of course, wish to distinguish between legitimate and illegitimate, between institutionalized and noninstitutionalized, kinship structures.

kinship units   Concrete structures (membership units) for which the membership criteria are oriented at least in part to biological descent and/or sexual intercourse.

latecomers   Those who become involved with a process after it has developed elsewhere. Frequently used with regard to modernization.

learning   Any increase in storage in the memory of an individual combined with ability to recall that which is stored.

learning, social   Any increase in storage in the memory, combined with the ability to recall that which is stored, that is not adequately explicable in terms of species' heredity and the nonspecies' environment at the present state of our knowledge about that heredity and that environment. For humans, social learning is any learning not adequately explicable in terms of human heredity and the nonhuman environment at our present state of knowledge about those categories.

logical action   See *rational action*.

magic   See *methodologically arational action*.

market   Any organization, however loosely organized, in terms of which action is primarily oriented to facilitating the exchange of goods and/or services among its members (or participants), with choice left up to them (i.e., with some degree(s) of freedom of choice).

mathematically stated (i.e., mathematical analysis)   A technique that, once a model for handling a problem has been defined, permits manipulation of the concepts involved without further reference to their substantive contents. Following Hermann Weyl. See *model*.

matriarchal   Any system in which, ideally and/or actually, political precedence is taken by females. Often alleged of families.

matriarchy   See *matriarchal*.

matrilineal   Any system in terms of which descent is reckoned in the female line. Usually said of families.

matrilineality   See *matrilineal*.

matrilocal

Any system in terms of which the residence is determined by residence of the female. Usually said of families.

matrilocality

See *matrilocal*.

means

Methods, materials, and services (i.e., a state of affairs) viewed as conducive to or necessary to achieve an end(s). N.B.: This usage must be distinguished from use of the term as equivalent to "explains," "indicates," etc. Thus, all means are meaningful, but not all meaningful things, ideas, or experiences are means. Some may be regarded as "ends in themselves."

medium of exchange

Any good or service that can be exchanged for two or more other goods and/or services. The more different items that a given article or service can be exchanged for, the more highly generalized it is as a medium of exchange.

member

See *membership*.

membership

The plurality of interacting individuals who are involved in a system of action by virtue of the fact that their action is primarily oriented to the system concerned, within the context concerned. The members of a society may, and commonly do today, vary in the extent to which they, either directly or indirectly, orient their actions to more than one such system of action. But they will be considered members of that society in terms of which their action is primarily oriented. Members of an organization may be more or less well integrated members of that organization, and they may be genuine members, as opposed to expedient members, of a given organization. *Genuine members°*, in fact, orient their action primarily to the system concerned within the context concerned; *expedient members*° do so only insofar as the appearance of such orientation is necessary for the achievement of other ends.

membership-criteria aspect   Describes the terms under which individuals are considered eligible or ineligible for inclusion in a relationship. See *membership*.

membership units   See *concrete structure*.

memory   "The power or function of reproducing and identifying what has been learned or experienced. This function includes learning, retention, recall, and recognition and is sometimes taken to include motor habits and skill." (*Webster's New International Dictionary*. 2d ed. G. & C. Merriam, 1954, p. 1534.)

merchant   Specialists in exchange, which in this sense is a special form of production focused on the service of distribution.

metaquestion   Any question whose answer falls within the realm of the presuppositions or a more general level of the subject under discussion.

methodologically arational action   Action for which the ends of the actor are empirical but the means are nonempirical, at least in part. Also used here as a definition of magic. Cf. *religion*.

model   A generalized description of a system of phenomena and/or concepts, as in mathematics and logic, that states the component parts of the system and at least some of the interrelationships of those component parts.

modernization (modern)   The level of modernization of any society is defined here by the ratio of inanimate to animate sources of energy used by the members of that society. A society will not be considered *relatively modernized* (or *modernized*) until that ratio is sufficiently high that comparatively small cutbacks in inanimate sources of energy cannot be made up or adjusted to without far-reaching changes in the social structures of the system at the most general level under consideration of that system.

modernization, high	The state of a society with high ratios of inanimate to animate sources of power whose members have developed mass markets for heavy consumer goods.
modernized society, relatively	Characterized by such high levels of the ratio of inanimate to animate sources of power that a comparatively small percentage of cutbacks in inanimate sources of power cannot be adjusted to without far-reaching social change at extremely general levels, if they can be adjusted to at all. Societies are never completely modernized or completely nonmodernized, but the term "relatively" may be dispensed with once this is clear.
moderns	People who orient their behavior to the patterns of modernization and at least to some extent accept them as institutionalized.
money	A legal or quasi-legal (or official or quasi-official) medium of exchange. In relatively modernized contexts, usually a single such medium is fixed upon, and that is legitimized and issued by the members of the government of the society concerned. Money is usually a highly generalized medium of exchange, and the more highly modernized societies become, the higher tends to be the level of generaliza-

tion of this medium of exchange. There can be no such thing as a completely generalized medium of exchange, i.e., a unit such that anything can be purchased in terms of it. This generalization will hold true despite the wisdom of cynics, past and present.

monism Any explanation for which all deductions or variations are seen as dependent functions of a single variable.

mother A female parent. One may distinguish between a puristically biologically defined mother—i.e., the female who actually conceives and bears a particular infant—and a socially defined one, i.e., any female defined as a mother by other individuals on the basis of puristically biologically defined criteria and/or other criteria. Despite the possibility of divergence, the ordinary expectation at all times in all known social contexts is that the two coincide.

mother surrogate One who performs the functions usually associated with a mother. Mother surrogates are usually female.

mother-time Time spent by mothers in direct contact with infants and young children. See *mother*.

motivation The establishment of the ends of action whether they are empirical or nonempirical, intermediate or ultimate.

multilineal conjugal family See *family, multilineal conjugal*.

multilineality Tracing descent through two or more lines.

neighborhood Concrete structures (or organizations or membership units) whose membership is determined at least in part by criteria of spatial proximity and which include as a minimum concrete substructures of other sorts.

neolocal   Pertaining to any system for which the determination of residence of the members is differentiated from any previous residence of any member. Neolocality may be an ideal/actual pattern.

neolocality   See *neolocal.*

nepotism   Any form of particularism oriented at least in part to kinship descent units and/or family units. By extension, the term in the vernacular has come to refer to particularism in general, much as the term "feudalism" has come to refer to any social system with a highly skewed distribution of income.

nonempirical   Residually defined relatively to empirical, i.e., not subject to sensory perception or to inference from sensory perception.

nonfamily units   Any kinship units other than family units and any nonkinship units. See *family.*

nonfamily units of Type I   Nonfamily units for which action is supposed to be (i.e., is ideally) affected by family considerations of the members.

nonfamily units of Type II   Nonfamily units for which action in terms of them is not supposed to be (i.e., is not ideally) affected by family considerations of the members.

nonhierarchical   The absence of differential rankings for members of a relationship.

nonkinship units   Concrete structures (or membership units) for which membership is oriented to neither biological descent nor sexual intercourse.

nonmodernized, relatively	Residual category of *modernized, relatively*. Refers to the vast majority of all societies, even today, and to all societies prior to the second third of the ninteenth century. See *modernized society, relatively*.
nonrational	All conscious action other than rational action.
nuclear family	See *family, conjugal*.
old age	That period of the life cycle during which, either by institutionalization of special privileges or by other means, the full responsibilities of adulthood are no longer expected of the individual who has passed through the period of adulthood. Old age is generally marked by some *rite de passage* such as a retirement ceremony based on age.
open class	A set of individuals with common characteristics that may be acquired after birth by achievement. A class system is considered to be more or less open to the extent that social barring is not an obstacle to class mobility.
organization	Any social system that may be characterized as having a membership. Any membership unit of a society, including a society itself.
parsimony	Logic. Economy of assumption in reasoning. (*Webster's New International Dictionary*. 2d ed. unabr., 1956 printing, p. 178)
particularism	Any application of criteria for a relationship that involves social barring and/or nongermaneness. There are three forms of particularism: 1. *germane* particularism involving social barring, but the social barring is relevant to the purposes of the relationship. 2. *capricious* particularism in-

volving no social barring, but the criteria are not germane to the relationship. 3. *ultimate* particularism involving both social barring and nongermaneness.

pathetic fallacy   The attribution of human qualities or capacities to nonhuman entities or phenomena. "The mountains pushed and the seas beckoned" is a classic use of the pathetic fallacy as a description of Japan as a setting for a society. "The system forced him to do it" is another ready example. *Systems of social action, as the terms are used here, do not do anything.* They consist only of patterns. *People do things to one another in terms of social systems.*

patriarchal   Any system in terms of which, ideally and/or actually, political precedence is taken by males. Often said of families.

patrilineal   Any system for which, ideally and/or actually, descent is reckoned in the male line; usually said of families.

patrilineality   See *patrilineal*.

patrilocal   Any system for which the residence is determined on the basis of where the male(s) reside; usually said of families.

patrilocality   See *patrilocal*.

pattern   Any conceptual and/or observable uniformity.

pleonasm   Redundancy. (*Webster's New International Dictionary*. 2d ed., 1956 printing, p. 1890) See *principle of pleonasm*.

political allocation   The distribution of power over, and responsibility for, the actions of the various members of the organization concerned, involving on the one hand the use of sanctions (of which force is the extreme form) in one direction, and on the other hand accountability to the members and in terms of the structure concerned or to the members of other concrete structures or to (from the point of view of the actor) nonempirical entities.

polyandry   Having to do with plural husbands.

polygamy   Having to do with plural spouses, either female or male.

polygyny   Having to do with plural wives.

power   The ability to exercise authority and/or control over the actions of others. More generally, the ability to influence the action of others.

prestige   Ascendancy derived from general admiration or esteem; commanding position in men's minds. (Quoted from *Webster's New International Dictionary.* 2d ed.)

primitive society   See *society, primitive.*

principle of parsimony   The principle that holds the simpler of two hypotheses with identical explanatory power is to be preferred in science. One of the metapropositions on which science rests. Also referred to as Ockham's Razor. See *parsimony.*

principle of pleonasm   The principle that holds that the more redundant an explanation the better. The term is polar to the principle of parsimony, a fundamental metaproposition of science. The fad for "thick description" in social analysis is the current favored form of the principle of pleonasm.

production   Those actions that result in an output of goods and/or services. There is, of course, some productive aspect of any action though that aspect may not be the relevant focus of attention.

production roles
Social positions differentiated on the basis of the output of goods and/or services.

puristically biological
Pertaining to any living phenomenon that can be adequately explained for purposes in hand solely in terms of the species' heredity and the nonspecies' .environment.

race
A social distinction, often applied invidiously to an individual or set of individuals on the basis of factors that are presumed to be biologically inherited by an individual or a set of individuals. The essence of the term when used as a basis for bigotry is social, not biological.

racism
Refers to the invidious application of the concept of race to an individual or set of individuals. See *race*.

rational action
Action for which the ends and the means are both empirical and the objective and subjective ends of action are identical; i.e., action for which the means chosen by the actor will in fact result in the actor achieving the ends sought. The term "rational" is here synonymous with logical, so correspondingly, are "nonrational," "irrational," and "arational" with "nonlogical," "illogical," and "alogical."

recreational
Pertaining to relaxation and release from the usual duties and concerns of daily life.

reduction
The explanation of phenomena usually considered on one level in terms of the constants and variables associated with a more general level. The explanation of

"social" phenomena in "psychological" or "biological" terms or of "biological" phenomena in molecular (chemical or physical) terms would be examples of reduction in science. The most elegant case of scientific reduction is the reduction of chemistry to a special case of physics via the discovery of the Periodic Table of Elements.

reify

To confuse an analytic structure (or distinction) with a concrete structure (or distinction), e.g., to regard "economic man" as "man."

relationship

In social analysis, any social structure (or set of structures) that defines the actions, ideally and actually, that determine the interdependence of two or more actors.

relative age

A distinction among individuals on the basis of their comparative ages.

relatively modernized society

See *modernized society, relatively*.

relatively nonmodernized society

See *nonmodernized, relatively*.

religion

A system of beliefs about action directly oriented to ultimate ends. See also *ultimately arational action*. Cf. *methodologically arational action* (magic).

religious

Having to do with action seen by the actor as directly oriented to ultimate ends. "Living a good life," "serving God," "being at one with the Cosmos" are all examples of religious action.

requisite patterns (or structures)

See *structural requisite*.

responsibility	The accountability of an individual(s) to other individuals or groups or nonempirical entities for his or her own acts and/or the acts of others.
responsible	A given relationship is more or less responsible to the degree that each of the parties to the relationship may be expected, in seeking to realize his or her own goals, to safeguard (even at the expense of some of his or her own goals) such goals of the other parties as are relevant to the relationship.
role	Any socially differentiated position.
role differentiation	Any distinction of heterogeneous roles. See *role*.
role model	Any actor perceived by any other actor to exemplify any socially differentiated position.
sanction	Penalty for nonconformity. See also *institution*.
schools	Predominantly educationally oriented concrete structures (membership units).
science	A set of generalized empirical propositions containing variables, preferably with deductive interdependencies among the members of the set, with the propositions of the set, at least in theory, subject to verification or disproof. A set of scientific propositions is vulnerable to either logical errors or empirical errors, i.e., errors of fact. The more abstract and parsimonious the set, the "better" it is in terms of the metapropositions that underlie science, as long as monisms are excluded. A perfect science, never yet approximated, would be a generalized empirical proposition

containing only two variables from which all other scientific propositions could be rigorously deduced. "Good" scientific theories are above all to be judged by their fruitfulness for the further development of scientific theories. A theory may prove to be highly fruitful even if it turns out to be empirically disproved as in the case of the Parity Principle in Physics. Short of a "perfect" scientific theory, one always expects any given theory to be disproved (i.e., contradicted or superseded), sooner or later, by a more parsimonious theory that explains more. Scientific propositions are not necessarily "better" than, say, "thick description." They're just wildly different.

self-sufficiency   A system of action in operation is in theory self-sufficient only if its members are, at least in theory, capable by their own actions of providing for all of the functional requisites of the system without interdependencies with the members of any other social system.

setting   Those factors that determine either exactly or on a probability basis the maximum range of possible variation in the patterns that characterize the unit for which those factors are said to constitute the setting.

sex   Biological distinction between males, females, and, rarely, mixed forms, about which there is some social patterning in terms of any and all societies.

sexual-
intercourse unit   Kinship structure (organization or membership unit) for which membership is determined by orientation, at least in part, to sexual intercourse.

social
: Any observable uniformity, artifact, idea, etc., associated with the individual(s) of any species that cannot be adequately explained for present purposes in terms of the species' heredity and the nonspecies' environment. For Homo sapiens these are, of course, human heredity and the nonhuman environment.

social action
: All action (i.e., operation, including mere persistence) by individuals of any given species that is explicable or analyzable in empirical terms and cannot be adequately explained for the purposes intended in terms of the species' heredity and the nonspecies' environment; i.e., for humans, in terms of human heredity and the nonhuman environment.

social change
: Any alteration in a system of action of a given species that is not adequately explicable solely in terms of the heredity of that species and its nonspecies' environment; i.e., for humans, in terms of human heredity and the nonhuman environment. See *change*.

social inertia
: The tendency of any social pattern to persist unless some specific social action is brought to bear on it.

socialization
: The inculcation of socially acceptable and unacceptable structures of action on an individual (or group). See *social*.

social learning
: See *learning, social*.

social structure
: Any observable set of uniformities (patterns) in terms of which an individual acts that are not adequately explicable for present purposes in terms of species' heredity and the nonspecies' environment.

social system   Any set of interdependent patterns defining the context of action for a plurality of interacting individuals who are the members of that social system (or concrete structure) that are not adequately explicable in terms of the species' heredity and the nonspecies' environment of the actors involved.

society   A system of social action in operation that (a) involves a plurality of interacting individuals of a given species (or group of species) whose actions are primarily oriented to the system concerned and who are recruited at least in part by the sexual reproduction of the members of the plurality involved; (b) is at least in theory self-sufficient for the action of this plurality; and (c) is capable of existing longer than the life span of an individual of the type(s) involved.

society, primitive   A society (1) whose membership is relatively small, making it possible for most of the members to be directly acquainted with most of the other members (perhaps even related to all of them by kinship ties of one sort or another); (2) for which the territory encompassed by the members at any given point in time is also relatively small; and (3) whose members live close to the bare margin of subsistence. *Primitive society* is a term more sinned against by social scientists than sinning.

sociobiologists   Scientists seeking to explain in terms of species' heredity and the nonspecies' environment the behavior of organisms currently regarded as not susceptible to such explanation. I.e., they try to reduce social phenomena to puristically biological explanations.

solidarity   Analytic structures (or patterns or aspects) in terms of which relationships are allocated according to the subcategories of content, strength, and intensity of the relationships.

specialized   Characteristic of only one or some subsets of a given set; i.e., not shared by all the members of a given social system.

specialized cognition   Knowledge not characteristic of all the members of a given set. What is ideally speaking basic knowledge for one society may be specialized knowledge for another. Only recently in human history, for example, has literacy come to be regarded as a basic form of cognition. For all societies, however, command of language is regarded as a basic form of cognition. Command of language is not basic for neonates but in one form or another comes to characterize them if they survive long enough and are not physically incapable of speaking or otherwise commanding a language.

stem family   See *family, stem.*

stranger   An individual previously unknown to the individual(s) with whom he (or she) comes in contact.

Strategic Research Material   "Strategic Research Sites, objects or events that exhibit the phenomena to be explained or interpreted to such advantage and in such accessible form that they enable the fruitful investigation of previously stubborn problems and the discovery of new problems for further inquiry" (Merton 1987, p. 12).

Strategic Research Site   A locus of Strategic Research Materials (following Merton 1987).

stratification	Role differentiation that distinguishes higher and lower standings or classifications in terms of one or more criteria.
stratification aspect	Having to do with hierarchical or non-hierarchical rankings of the members of any relationship. See *stratification*.
strength	The relative precedence or lack thereof taken by a given relationship (or factor) over other relationships (or factors) of its general sort and over other obligations and commitments in any larger social sphere.
structural prerequisite	A structure that must exist if action in terms of it is to result in the functional prerequisites of any given unit. N.B.: To maintain that any given structure must exist or does exist because it is a structural prerequisite of a given unit is to commit a form of structural teleology, in this case, structural prerequisite teleology.
structural requisite	A pattern or observable uniformity of action or operation necessary for the continued existence of the unit with which it is associated given the level of generalization of the definition of the unit and the most general setting of such a unit. N.B.: To state that a structure exists (or must exist) because it is a structural requisite is to commit a form of *structural teleology*°, in this case, structural requisite teleology.
structural teleology	The fallacy of attributing the existence of a structure to any function produced in terms of it; e.g., families exist to socialize children. See *functional teleology*. The hypothesis that actors orient their behavior to future states of affairs is not teleological in this sense. It is currently an essential tool of social analysis.

structure	A pattern, any observable uniformity of action or operation. N.B.: Structure from one point of view is a function from another. The structure of a child's behavior may be "politeness"; that same "politeness," however, is also a function of the socialization of the child by parents. See *function*.
substantive-definition aspect	Having to do with the activities or considerations or rights and obligations or performances that are covered by a relationship. Used here particularly with regard to the precision of definition and delimitations of the rights and obligations of the individuals involved.
system	Any patterned collection of elements.
system of theory	A set of generalized statements containing variables that are all to some degree more or less well integrated with one another, i.e., more or less interdependent. See *system* and *theory*.
tabula rasa	"The smooth tablet; hence the mind before receiving impressions from without . . . ." (*Webster's New International Dictionary*. 2d ed.) Vulgarly, but usefully, referred to as a "blank mind."
tautological	Explained solely in terms of itself, not conceivably falsifiable. Such statements are considered inutile in any empirical science, though they are of the essence in mathematics and logic.
teaching	The inculcation of learning.
teleology	The attribution of purpose. For science, the attribution of purpose as an explanation for a phenomenon is regarded as a fallacy.

theoretical system   Sets of theories with more or less powerful deductive interdependencies. See *system of theory*.

theory   A generalized statement containing variables. Empirical scientific theories are generalized statements containing variables that utilize concepts having empirical referents and draw empirical relationships between (or among) referents of two or more such concepts. Empirical scientific theories are vulnerable both to logical errors and errors about observable phenomena.

thick description   A concept usually left undefined or defined only by example. It represents a replacement of the principle of parsimony by the principle of pleonasm. Apparently an event or scene is "thickly described" if one piles up enough descriptive material until "the meaning comes" to the observer. (Thorstein Veblen once teased a pious and devout student who greatly admired Veblen's command of German and asked how he had acquired it. "I stared at the words," said Veblen, "until the meanings came to me.") Implicit in this concept is the idea that a parsimonious description is incapable of conveying the essence of the situation. Thick description is a basic tool in our new anti-intellectualism. It occupies a pole opposite to that of science, for which denotation is everything and connotation is a curse. In terms of thick description, denotation, if it can be achieved at all, can only be achieved by a piling up, as it were, of connotative anecdotes. Thick descriptions cannot be generalized. Who is to say whether thick descriptions are right or wrong, tenable or untenable, fruitful or barren?

traditional An institutionalization that serves to perpetuate an institution. All institutions are to some extent traditionalized. There are, thus, no nontraditional or untraditional societies or social systems, because all social systems involve some institutions, however specialized. N.B.: Modernized (relatively modernized) societies are not "nontraditional," "untraditional," or "atraditional." In some respects, but by no means in all, traditions in modernized societies are different, and have a different position in general social structure, from those of nonmodernized societies.

ultimate ends Ends that are not viewed as means for any other ends; i.e., ends that are ends in themselves.

ultimately arational action Action for which both the ends and means of the actor are at least in part nonempirical; e.g., religion as defined here. Cf. *methodologically arational action* (magic).

ultimate particularism Membership criteria that involve both social barring and nongermaneness.

uncertainty situations Situations in which unanticipated factors are relevant, whether recognized or not.

universalistic Pertaining to membership criteria such that no one is socially barred from being a party to the relationship and such that the criteria are themselves germane to the purposes for which the selection is made. What is generally described as *meritocratic* is what is here meant by universalistic or predominantly universalistic.

universals Relative to any set, universals are those elements, aspects, etc., that apply to any and all members of the set.

ur	Primeval, aboriginal.
ur relationships	Aboriginal relationships.
utopian pattern	An ideal pattern of a sort with which general conformity is not expected (i.e., is not institutionalized), but one that may be institutionalized and traditionalized as an ideal pattern. Utopian patterns are ones for which respect in moral terms is usually institutionalized and traditionalized, even though the very people who hold them so do not regard them as realistic expectations. Utopian patterns are probably vital as a first step in socializing individuals, especially children, in terms of complex institutions. Thus, we often tell children they should "never tell a lie," distinguishing later between acceptable and unacceptable levels of lying; e.g., the concept of the "little white lie."
vicarious participation	Involvement by the actor(s) via spectator or observer roles.
world system	Any set of social systems on planet Earth with interdependencies among those systems. Such systems can indeed be tenuous ones, characterized by very modest levels of interdependence. Exaggeration of those interdependencies is a persistent characteristic of "it's a plot" theories of international (or intersocietal, or intercultural) phenomena.
young children	Children up to three, four, or five years of age. See *childhood*.

References

Alexander, Jeffrey C. 1982. *Theoretical Logic in Sociology*. Berkeley and Los Angeles: University of California Press.

Bachofen, Johann J. 1861. *Das Mutterrecht*. Basel: Beno Schwebe.

Cazeneuve, Jean. 1968. "Levy-Bruhl." *International Encyclopedia of the Social Sciences*, 9:265. New York: Macmillan and Free Press.

Chodorow, Nancy. 1978. *The Reproduction of Mothering: Psychoanalysis and the Sociology of Gender*. Berkeley and Los Angeles: University of California Press.

Chuang-tzu. 1986. *The Inner Chapters*. Translated by Angus C. Graham. London: George Allen and Unwin.

Coale, Ansley, Paul Demeny, and Barbara Vaughn. 1983. *Regional Life Tables and Stable Populations*. 2d ed. New York: Academic Press.

Coale, Ansley, Lloyd A. Fallers, Marion J. Levy, Jr., David M. Schneider, and Sylvan S. Tomkins. 1965. *Aspects of the Analysis of Family Structure*. Princeton: Princeton University Press.

Dinnerstein, Dorothy. 1976. *The Mermaid and the Minotaur: Sexual Arrangements and Human Malaise*. New York: Harper and Row.

Durkheim, Emile. 1932. *De la division du travail social*. 6th ed. Paris: Felix Aleca.

Feynman, Richard P. 1985. *Surely You're Joking, Mr. Feynman!* New York: W. W. Norton.

Flavell, John H. 1963. *The Developmental Psychology of Jean Piaget.* Princeton: Princeton University Press.

Geertz, Clifford. 1973. *The Interpretation of Cultures.* New York: Basic Books.

Hrdy, Sarah B. 1981. *The Woman That Never Evolved.* Cambridge: Harvard University Press.

Hsu, F. L. K., ed. 1971. *Kinship and Culture.* Chicago: Aldine.

Kluckhohn, Clyde. 1973. "Bronislaw Malinowski, 1884–1942." *Journal of American Folklore* 56 (July–September): 214.

Kochen, M., and Marion J. Levy, Jr. 1956. "The Logical Nature of an Action Scheme." *Behavioral Science* 1, (October): 265–89.

Konner, M. J. *See* West, Mary M., and Melvin J. Konner.

Kunstadter, Peter, Roald Buhler, Fred Stephan, and Charles Westoff. 1963. "Demographic Variability and Preferential Marriage Patterns." *American Journal of Physical Anthropology* 21 (December): 511–19.

Lancaster, Jane. 1973. "In Praise of the Achieving Female Monkey." *Psychology Today* (September): 30, 32, 34–36, 99.

Law, William. [1762] 1893. *The Works of the Reverend William Law, M.A., Sometime Fellow of Emmanuel College, Cambridge.* 9 vols. Printed for J. Richardson. Privately reprinted for C. Moreton Setley, Brockenhurst, New Forest, Hampshire.

Levy, Marion J., Jr. 1949. *The Family Revolution in Modern China.* Cambridge: Harvard University Press.

———. 1981. *Levy's Eleven Laws of the Disillusionment of the True Liberal.* 5th ed. Princeton: Princeton University Press.

———. 1970. *Modernization and the Structure of Societies.* Princeton: Princeton University Press.

———. 1952. *The Structure of Society.* Princeton: Princeton University Press.

Levy-Bruhl, Lucien. 1926. *How Natives Think.* London: Allen and Unwin. First published as *Les fonctions mentales dans les sociétés inférieures.* Paris: F. Alcan, 1910.

———. 1923. *Primitive Mentality.* New York: Macmillan. First published as *La mentalité primitive.* Paris: Presses universitáires de France, 1922.

———. 1935. *Primitives and the Supernatural.* New York: Dutton. First published as *Le surnaturel et la nature dans la mentalité primitive.* Paris: F. Alcan, 1931.

Machlup, Fritz. 1962. *The Production and Distribution of Knowledge in the United States*. Princeton: Princeton University Press.

Malinowski, Bronislaw K. 1922. *Argonauts of the Western Pacific*. London: Routledge and Kegan Paul.

———. 1948. *Magic, Science, and Religion and Other Essays*. Glencoe: Free Press.

Merton, Robert K. 1972. "Insiders and Outsiders: A Chapter in the Sociology of Knowledge." *American Journal of Sociology* 78 (July): 9–47.

———. 1987. "Three Fragments from a Sociologist's Notebooks: Establishing the Phenomena, Specified Ignorance, and Strategic Research Materials." *Annual Review of Sociology* 13:1–28.

Montessori, Maria. 1964. *The Montessori Method*. Cambridge, Eng.: Bentley.

Parsons, Talcott. 1949. *Essays in Sociological Theory: Pure and Applied*. Glencoe: Free Press.

———. 1937. *The Structure of Social Action*. New York: McGraw-Hill.

Piaget, Jean. 1959. *The Language and Thought of the Child*. 3d ed., rev. New York: Humanities Press. First published as *Le langage et la pensée chez l'enfant*. 1923. Neuchâtel, Paris: Delachaux and Niestle.

———. 1952. *The Origins of Intelligence in Children*. New York: International Universities Press. First published as *La naissance de l'intelligence chez l'enfant*, 1936. Neuchâtel: Delachaux and Niestle.

Roget, Peter M. 1937. *Thesaurus of English Words and Phrases*. American ed. New York: Grosset and Dunlap. Enlarged by J. L. Roget, revised and enlarged by S. R. Roget.

Schneider, David M., and Kathleen Gough. 1961. *Matrilineal Kinship*. Berkeley and Los Angeles: University of California Press.

Thomas, William I., and Dorothy S. Thomas. 1928. *The Child in America*. New York: Alfred A. Knopf.

Tomkins, Sylvan S. 1962. *Affect, Imagery, Consciousness*. New York: Springer.

Turnbull, Colin. 1972. *The Mountain People*. New York: Simon and Schuster.

Twain, Mark. 1897. *Following the Equator*. New York: Harper and Bros.

West, Mary M., and Melvin J. Konner. 1976. "The Role of the Father: An Anthropological Perspective." In *The Role of the Father in Child Development,* edited by M. E. Lamb. New York: John Wiley and Son.

Westermarck, Edward. 1891. *The History of Human Marriage*. London: MacMillan.

Index

Compositor:	Interactive Composition Corporation
Text:	11/13 Bembo
Display:	Bembo
Printer:	Maple-Vail Book Mfg. Group
Binder:	Maple-Vail Book Mfg. Group